W9-CRO-173

Irresistible!
Markets, Models,
and Meta-Value in
Consumer Electronics

Irresistible! Markets, Models, and Meta-Value in Consumer Electronics

George Bailey and Hagen Wenzek

IBM Press
Pearson plc

Upper Saddle River, NJ • Boston • Indianapolis • San Francisco
New York • Toronto • Montreal • London • Munich • Paris • Madrid
Capetown • Sydney • Tokyo • Singapore • Mexico City

www.ibmpressbooks.com

IBM Press Program Manager: Tara Woodman, Ellice Uffer
IBM Press Consulting Editor: Karen Keeter
Cover design: IBM Corporation
Published by Pearson plc
Publishing as IBM Press

Library of Congress Cataloging-in-Publication Data

Irresistible electronics / George Bailey, Hagen Wenzek (eds.).
   p. cm.
Includes bibliographical references.
ISBN 0-13-198758-5 (hardback : alk. paper)
1. Electronic industries. 2. Electronic industries—Technological innovations. 3. Household electronics. I. Bailey, George. II. Wenzek, Hagen.

HD9696.A2I77 2005
338.4'762138—dc22

2005027592

ISBN 0-13-198758-5
Text printed in the United States on recycled paper at R. R. Donnelley in Crawfordsville, Indiana
First printing, December, 2005

Dedication

This book is dedicated to our clients in the electronics industry, who are changing the way we live by changing the way they work.

Contents

Preface

We have worked with many, if not most, of the leader-ship teams of major consumer electronics (CE) companies around the world. To say that these teams are in a state of flux falls short of describing the changes they are facing and the decisions they must make. They know we are entering an incredible period of growth, a period when consumer electronics will change the world we live in and how we live in it. It is also a period that the consumer electronics companies understand what they must be prepared for. Their current business models will most probably limit their opportunities, and unless they change, many will not thrive and some may not survive. Although all the CE companies are struggling to find the way forward, this is all new, and there are few definitive answers. After working with our clients everywhere from Helsinki to Osaka to New York, we decided to collect and share some of the insights we have gained. One word about IBM, considering we both work for IBM: IBM is not a CE company and doesn't plan to become one. Instead we are the "arms supplier" to the industry. We provide technology, business advice, and software to virtually all the ecosystem players.

This book is intended to be of interest to the millions of consumers who are fascinated by CE and who are curious about where things are going. The book is intended to be essential reading to the thousands of CE industry executives and the executives of adjacent companies who either buy, distribute, or contribute products to CE companies.

We look forward to working with our clients on creating the future of consumer electronics and discussing with all of you at the next opportunity.

George Bailey—Global Electronics Industry Leader, IBM Business Consulting Services, Greenwich, CT, USA, December 2005

Hagen Wenzek—Global Electronics Industry Leader, IBM Institute for Business Value, Heidelberg, Germany, December 2005

Find additional insight at www.ibm.com/industries/electronics/irresistible.

Acknowledgments

We would like to send our special thanks for their support and contribution to:

Linda Ban

Jörg Freienstein

Allan Henderson

Sean Lafferty

Kevin Reardon

Lisa Smith

and all the clients who worked with us to define the future of consumer electronics.

About the Authors

Akihiro Horibe. Technical Expert and research staff member at the IBM Research Laboratory, Tokyo, Japan.

Albert Li. Partner at IBM Business Consulting Services and Industrial Sector Executive of IBM Greater China Group, Shanghai, China.

Allan Henderson. Global leader for learning and knowledge management in the electronics industry of IBM, Atlanta, GA, USA.

Andreas Neus. Senior Consultant for strategy and change management in the communications industry with IBM Business Consulting Services, Hamburg, Germany.

Brigitte Majewski. Associate Director of marketing strategy at Modem Media, a Digitas company. Former consultant for strategy and change at IBM Business Consulting Services, Cambridge, MA, USA.

Charles B. Whinney, IV. Consultant for American Express Tax and Business Services Inc.'s National Business Consulting Practice, Villanova, PA, USA.

Christian Schiller. IT Architect for pervasive and wireless solutions at IBM Business Consulting Services, Heidelberg, Germany.

Derk Frank. Medical doctor, clinical resident, and research fellow in internal medicine/cardiology at the University hospital, Heidelberg, Germany.

George Bailey. Global Lead Partner for the electronics industry consulting practice at IBM Business Consulting Services, Greenwich, CT, USA.

Hagen Wenzek. Global Leader for the electronics industry research practice of the Institute for Business Value at IBM Business Consulting Services, Heidelberg, Germany.

Iris Ginzburg. Global Leader for the innovation management practice at IBM Research, Haifa, Israel.

Jim Kahle. IBM Fellow and Chief Architect and Director of Technology for the Austin-based design centre for the Cell Technology, Austin, TX, USA.

Kevin Reardon. General Manager of IBM Global Electronics Industry, White Plains, NY, USA.

Lisa Su. Vice President of Technology Development and Alliances in the IBM Systems and Technology Group, Fishkill, NY, USA.

Mike West. MultiMedia Architect for Pervasive Computing at IBM Systems Technology Group, Burlington, VA, USA.

Nancy M. Forbes. Manager of the IBM Headlights Program, Atlanta, GA, USA.

Nobuhiro Asai. Senior Manager for Pervasive Computing Architectures at IBM Software Group, Yamato, Japan.

Norishige Morimoto. Senior Manager for Science and Technology in the Tokyo Laboratories of IBM Research, Tokyo, Japan.

Paul Brody. Associate Partner for Supply Chain Management in the electronics industry practice at IBM Business Consulting Services, San Francisco, CA, USA.

Ralf Baral. Global Leader for Business Development in Asset Monitoring at IBM Business Consulting Services, Stuttgart, Germany.

Robin Williams. Associate Lab Director at the IBM Research Centre, Almaden, CA, USA.

Sean Lafferty. Global Leader of On Demand Solutions in the electronics industry practice at IBM Business Consulting Services, New York, NY, USA.

Stephen J. Andriole. Professor of Decision and Information Technologies in Villanova University's College of Commerce and Finance, Villanova, PA, USA.

Tom Osterday. Managing Principal for Electronic Design Technology Solutions at IBM Engineering and Technology Services, Phoenix, AZ, USA.

Yossi Lichtenstein. Manager for Innovation Management at the IBM Research Laboratories, Haifa, Israel.

About the Editors

George Bailey is IBM's Global Managing Partner for the Electronics industry consulting practice and a member of IBM's senior leadership team. In this role, Mr. Bailey is responsible for managing over several billion of IBM's business within the Electronics industry, which encompasses clients in consumer electronics, semiconductor, and telecommunications equipment manufacturing sectors, among others. Mr. Bailey leads a global network of thousands of employees focused on the Electronics industry, helping companies transform innovative ideas into bold, meaningful actions that drive business success and enhance enterprise value for our clients.

Mr. Bailey is an internationally recognized authority on strategic change and has led large-scale, multi-year transformational projects for progressive global companies. He is a sought-after speaker and has published numerous books, articles, and white papers.

Mr. Bailey received an M.A. from Pepperdine University and a M.B.A. from Drucker School of Management at Claremont College. He resides in Greenwich, Connecticut with his wife and four children. He won his division in the 1995 Transpacific yacht race and remains an avid sailor.

Dr. Hagen Wenzek is the Global Leader for the Electronics industry at the IBM Institute for Business Value (IBV). In this role, Dr. Wenzek is responsible for developing and deploying thought leadership in the Electronics industry. He generates the industry insight in the think tank environment of the IBV, in close collaboration with IBM account teams, clients, and academia, such as the Harvard Business School.

In his role as an Associate Partner for IBM Business Consulting Services, Dr. Wenzek has the additional responsibility to engage Electronics industry clients. He has led global consulting engagements from large transformation projects to focused strategy projects. Furthermore, Dr. Wenzek presents the results of his work at international conferences and in lectures at renowned universities.

Dr. Wenzek received a Diploma in Electrical Engineering from Aachen University and a Doctoral Degree in Electrical Engineering from Hagen University, both in Germany. He lives in Heidelberg, where he trains to participate in swimming, running, and cycling competitions.

Irresistible Electronics, Turbulent Times

George Bailey, Hagen Wenzek

Consumer electronics (CE) are irresistible. There is nothing quite so fascinating as seeing someone else use a new gadget for the first time. We can't help but wonder how that gadget could improve our own lives. Whether it's music or sports on the go, uninterrupted access to friends and family, or more life-like entertainment in the home, new consumer technology sparks the imagination like nothing else.

It is no surprise then that Consumer Electronics revenue is soaring. The CEA estimates that CE will top $130 billion in the U.S. in 2006 and grow more than 2 times the current rate of GDP growth in the U.S. over the next four years.[1] CE companies continue to raise the bar of consumer expectations by driving out new innovations at an increasingly perilous pace. Perilous to profits that is. Despite the rapid revenue expansion,

---

1. Consumer Electronics Association, members.ce.org/MarketResearch/cefuture.aspx, CE Future Forecast Database: members.ce.org/MarketResearch/Default.aspx, Market Research, CE Future.

CE companies still have not captured the margins of a hot growth industry. Further, the revenue is still spurred by those "technology hungry customers"[2] and not by the service-sensitive, smart shopper who is emerging and expected to dominate the future market. That bigger cake is also being eaten by more players—players from outside of the traditional realm of consumer electronics, such as Apple, Dell, and Microsoft®. A closer look at today's financial picture supports the case for change. "We don't make money, but we have fun!"[3] What Larry Mondry, CEO of CompUSA, cynically says about the PC business is sadly quite true for the CE industry.

Even with a continuing stream of innovations, the average price has remained quite stable (about US $184 per unit).[4] Average earnings margins (EBIT) in 2004 ranged between 0.4 percent for photographic equipment and 3.1 percent for white goods.[5] Compare that to medical device manufacturers that enjoyed a margin of more than 12 percent in 2004.[6]

Consumers are adopting new technologies—from music players to digital cameras and electronic healthcare devices—at astounding rates. Industry revenue is hitting all-time highs. For an industry exploding with demand, much of the enthusiasm is tempered by the lack of profits. It's a conundrum that is difficult to explain. How can we be experiencing a renaissance period of growth and rapid adoption of innovative technology but still lack real profits?

Clearly, such turbulent times indicate the need for a paradigm shift, as traditional business models are not providing adequate returns. CE companies need to think differently—and about things they haven't focused on in the past. For instance, today's

---

2. Ibid.
3. Smith, Steve. "CompUSA's Mondry's Goals and Opinions on CE Market." *TWICE*, June 29, 2005.
4. IBM analysis of "Electronic Equipment Factory Production Data by Application Market: Q2 2005 WW AMFT - Consumption Forecast." iSuppli Corporation, www.isuppli.com/marketwatch/default.asp?id=160.
5. IBM analysis of public company data, 2003 and 2004.
6. Ibid.

CE environment requires companies to be more responsive to the consumer. Fixed cost structures need to become variable to adapt to rapid growth. Innovation that matters must drive market leadership. We must focus on a new set of strategies to succeed.

Industry insiders have long been predicting fantastic, futuristic images of cars communicating with toasters and digital music flying around the home. But, as Thoreau said of the early buzz surrounding the Maine-Texas electromagnetic telegraph in the 1840's, "Maine and Texas, it may be, have nothing important to communicate."[7] While it might be easy to dismiss that notion today, it is quite possible that there were no profits to be made with the telegraph in 1845. Today, while cars may not have anything important to communicate to toasters, what keeps music from floating freely about our homes is not a lack of profits, but rather the players' traditional business models.

Across the globe, the IBM consumer electronics industry team is working with leading CE companies to develop the new business models that will excel in today's industry landscape. We call such a company an "On Demand Business." Soon, we believe the industry will be calling these innovators "the winners."

THE THREE M'S

The critical elements contributing to growth and innovation in this emerging turbulent world are categorized by the three M's: Meta-value, Models, and Markets. *Meta-value* is the idea that the convergence and integration of technologies, devices, services, and content go beyond synergy. Just as important as the new technologies that are enabling meta-value, are new *models* for doing business. And finally, growth and innovation is being fueled by new geographic *markets*, especially the BRIC countries (Brazil, Russia, India, and China).

---

7. Thoreau, Henry David. *Walden*. Researched in www.online-literature.com/
    thoreau/walden/.

META-VALUE: GAINING FAR MORE THAN A SUM OF PARTS

Synergy is the dated concept that $1 + 1 = 3$, implying that the combination of two things provides more than additive value. By contrast, meta-value is the notion that by combining two things, you can get completely different, emergent properties. For instance, combining two hydrogen atoms with an oxygen atom doesn't create three atoms, it creates wetness. In CE, new technologies are enabling meta-value, where new combinations of products, content, and services are creating emergent properties for the end consumer. Meta-value is being enhanced particularly in the areas of telehealthcare, gaming, and Smart Homes and supported by innovative technologies such as the Cell processor™ and Linux®.

TELEHEALTHCARE: BEYOND MERGING HOMES WITH HOSPITALS

Medical devices—where the high margins reside—and CE *are* converging at the home: *Telehealthcare* brings sophisticated medical treatment to the patient's house with the chance to drive down healthcare system costs and improve well-being at the same time. With telehealthcare, for instance, people with congestive heart failure may leave the hospital earlier because the doctors can monitor their status remotely. They may live longer, as a deterioration of health can ideally be noticed before a state of emergency occurs (see Chapter 5, "Telehealthcare: The Key to the Living Room," for more details). It will be hard to resist such a value proposition, especially if prescribed by a medical doctor.

Not only is technology converging, but whole worlds are merging. The world of medical care now reaches the home not only through nurses, but through a TV, a mobile phone, or an Internet browser. This is all happening in a sensitive area under strict control, but it is finally happening. The focus is primarily on elderly people, who tend to suffer most from chronic diseases.

GAMING: WHEN PLAY SEEMS VERY REAL

If the purpose is fun, the other end of the age spectrum gets interested. In fact, online gaming is displacing many of the traditional things people do in their spare time, like watching TV (see Chapter 6, "Online Gaming Environments: People, Technology, Money, and Social Networks," for more details). This has led to a market whose size is expected to exceed some US $30 billion for computer and videogames in 2007.[8]

The tagline for a 1983 movie, "Is it a game or is it real?"[9] could describe today's daily entertainment. Just as vital parameters are captured from a patient's body to feed a medical system, real-time telematics from a Formula 1 race can be added to a racing game, or actual flight control data can be combined with the environment of a flight simulator.

In gaming, the fight for the CE market becomes very apparent: Microsoft against Sony—the Xbox against the PlayStation. Will the winner be the software company that uses its full power to first capture the young and then overtake more of the CE market? Or can the incumbent regain its strength by leveraging its brand and the content it owns?

SMART HOMES: SETTING UP GREATER CONVENIENCE, INNOVATION

While archaic CE business models have been slow to unlock *technology convergence* into the *Smart Home*, maybe we have been searching in the wrong place for the key. Maybe the "key to the home is through the heart," said George Pohle, Vice President of the IBM Institute for Business Value, the IBM think tank for Business Consulting Services. The way these medical and gaming services are defined, for example, can also determine how subsequent Smart Home services will be offered.

TECHNOLOGIES THAT UNDERPIN META-VALUE CREATION

Once a platform has found its way into the living room, the base technology is there to provide more services, whether for healthcare, security, convenience, or fun. So CE companies from all

---

8. "Video Game Industry," RocResearch, 2004-05.
9. "War Games," movie by John Badham, 1983.

areas are readjusting their business models or developing completely new ones to define, offer, and deliver those life-enhancing services.

CELL PROCESSOR: PUMPING UP THE POWER

Driving the incredibly real animations of a modern game on small and cheap consoles is computing power unlike any seen before. The ten-fold increase the Cell processor brings to game consoles is also attractive for a wealth of new CE applications (see Chapter 7, "The Soul of the Next Generation of Consumer Electronics Products," for more detail). As new ecosystems are formed around them, these applications will push the limits of emerging business models. The trick is discerning which will be the profitable ones.

LINUX EVERYWHERE: THE POSSIBILITIES OF OPEN SOURCE

One of the predictions made a couple of years ago was that open source software, especially in its manifestation as Linux, would revamp the industry. In a heterogeneous computing environment, CE companies not running some of their servers with Linux can expect to be questioned at length. Choosing open source software for mission-critical business applications might elicit prolonged discussions in corporate IT departments, but for the youth-fueled start-ups of today, the decision is a "no-brainer." Just as Aaron Levie, CEO of Box.net, "assesses the attitude of his fellow 20-something entrepreneurs: 'My extended network is all in the younger crowd. I don't know anyone who's not developing on Linux.'"[10]

This same technology is now moving to the device level (see Chapter 9, "Embedded Linux: For Embedded Systems Today and Into the Future," for more detail). Linux enters the stage to become the operating system of choice for mobile phones, PDAs, home gateways, or wristwatches. It is robust, it is secure, it is

---

10. Hellweg, Eric. "The Tech Boom 2.0," *Technology Review.com*, August 12, 2005.

fast—and it is free! If you are following the fierce battle between Symbian, BlackBerry, Palm OS, and Windows® CE, you can sit back and relax. Without much fuss, CE Linux is expected to sneak in and take over a growing share of the market. Facing razor-thin margins, finding a way to cut out costs can push more CE companies toward Linux.

MODELS: OPTIMIZING THE CE BUSINESS MODEL

The traditional business model, observed in the overwhelming majority of our clients, has two notable flaws: It is siloed by nature, and it lacks focus on differentiating, core activities. Siloed business units with individual profit-and-loss measurements, as opposed to a company-wide view, are preventing the kind of solution-oriented focus that leads to breakthrough innovations that matter to the consumer. In the traditional model, CE companies streamline functions under each product line chief. Chiefs of different product-aligned divisions are so focused on their own responsibilities that they frequently are unaware of what other product divisions are doing.

The second flaw in the traditional business model is the lack of focus on what really matters. We would not suggest that the industry centralize or outsource all components of its diverse businesses. Rather, by viewing an enterprise as a collection of interlocking business components, industry players will be able to focus on their core competencies, and then form teams across divisions on specific business components to drive costs out of the business. This is the key concept behind IBM Component Business Modelling (CBM), and it is already beginning to take shape across the industry.

The new paradigm in business models is focused and responsive. Companies such as Apple and Samsung are eschewing traditional business models and leaving them in the dust. Over the last four years, Apple's stock price has climbed more than 300 percent and Samsung's more than 150 percent, while traditional CE powerhouses have lost 10 to 50 percent of their stock prices in the same period.[11] The CE companies experiencing gains have fueled growth and innovation by focusing on what matters and excelling in those core capabilities, like product design, branding, and maintaining consumer relationships.

In the last several years, we have seen many players in the CE market undertake a major transformation initiative. And each has recognized the lack of integration and innovative teaming across product lines and divisions. Still many struggle to overcome the internal politics that reinforce the powerful barriers of entrenched business models. Tomorrow's winners will find ways to break down the barriers to change and will team—both internally and externally—to drive to the consumer innovative solutions that matter.

CUSTOMER RELATIONSHIP MANAGEMENT: CONSUMERS AND CE

As the big retailers grow larger, they catch more and more of the consumer relationship. And the consumer knows every product and price and comments about it from the Internet. Only the CE company now knows increasingly less about its customers. This seriously impacts the optimal strategy regarding sales channels, partnering approaches, branding, and so forth because strategy has to depend on what the customers want (see Chapter 12, "Consumer Relationships: A Tale of Channels and Brands" for more detail). The CE companies must find ways to engage the end customer directly and capture data about its customers. This is one way to build institutional knowledge about the customer.

The data to help build that knowledge may already exist—and may already be inside the company, from loyalty cards, RFID tags, and consumer complaints. But it takes systems, people, and processes, to make sense of that plain data and transform it into information that then forms the basis for those strategic decisions. Unfortunately, few CE companies currently have that full capability.

An offshoot of customer relationship management (CRM) happens when leading-edge companies leave innovation to the customer,

---

11. Company financial reports.

using the approach MIT professor Eric von Hippel calls "democra-tizing innovation."[12] Here, the manufacturer acknowledges that suppliers and complementors are part of its value network and can run parts of its business better than the manufacturer itself. Also the customer might take over a critical piece of the business model. The so-called "lead-user" knows better than anybody else, includ-ing the manufacturer, what he or she wants. For 3M, applying this method led to "more than eight times the sales forecast [than] for new products developed in the traditional manner."[13] Even though it "is painful and difficult for many manufacturers"[14] to make that transition, it is another chance to avoid being one of those many CE companies that will fade away in the next few years.

COMPONENT BUSINESS MODELLING: FINDING THE DIFFERENTIATORS

Recognizing CRM as a key component in CE enterprises is just one way to identify differentiators using Component Business Modelling. Often, what can be removed from a business model can make it more successful. CE companies have squeezed performance out of the finished goods supply chain and are now looking toward the service supply chain as the next frontier for competitive advantage.

But this has not been an easy task for the traditional CE compa-nies. Many years of focusing on products and product innovation have entrenched a strong product engineering culture into the tra-ditional CE players. Many of them do not have the capabilities in house to focus on developing service offerings. Even worse is the fact that many do not fully understand which capabilities they need and which they have. It is extremely difficult to drive a trans-formation of this kind when you don't know where you are, and you're not exactly sure where you're going.

Through CBM, a CE company can adjust its business model to determine the most efficient and profitable ways of performing

---

12. von Hippel, Eric, "Democratizing Innovation," MIT Press, Cambridge, MA, 2005.
13. Ibid.
14. Ibid.

various business functions. Typically, by concentrating internally on those parts of the business that provide a competitive advantage, CE companies can benefit from looking externally for resources to perform functions such as travel expense management, human resources back office, and indirect material procurement. Instead of basing such decisions on gut feelings, CBM enables fact-based decisions to design the business model in a way that reflects strategy.

To illustrate, CBM enables the flexibility to shape the whole business model according to the customer demand and partner supply: Reverse logistics? Leave that to the logistics specialist for x Euros per device. Installation? The local expert does it for y Euros less. Billing? The shared services centre eliminates x Euros from the budget. Design? It is a core competency with y full-time people.

Using a disaggregated business model, one can actually do a bottom-up calculation of the entire business case for a new product, directly describing the market potential in relation to the enterprise's capabilities—and stealing the thunder from those who tend to defer decisions. You can finally hope to hit the market at the right time, with the right solution, at the right price. You "just" have to know what the customer wants—and how to structure the business optimally to provide it.

PARTNERSHIPS LEAD TO SUCCESS

This business model optimization will likely drive an industry consolidation as emerging technologies continue to drive previously unthinkable partnerships and joint ventures that will eventually lead to more mergers and acquisitions. In the white goods industry this consolidation is already in full swing: While Whirlpool acquires Maytag to succeed in the mature U.S. market, Toshiba is going for a joint venture with TCL to capture a piece of the growing market in China.

This is just one example of how the leaders and survivors are taking advantage of partnerships as part of their new business models. Based on IBM client experience, just to survive, those that remain will also have transformed about half of their fixed costs to variable costs and cut the costs of selling their goods by an average of one-third. This is because revenue volatility within the industry has greatly exceeded the variability of the cost structure, leading to unpredictable quarterly profit results. Operations need to become much more efficient and innovation highly effective. There is no way to remain viable when writing off a huge part of all inventories year after year or missing the market window for the latest innovation all the time. In fact, we believe that a quarter of all companies in the CE market today may not last another five years. They will either abandon the market, like Thomson selling its final piece of CE "to focus on [...] media services, systems, and equipment technology,"[15] or be acquired and cease to exist.

And all of this will work only if the companies do the opposite of what such a fierce battle reflexively implies: Build trust throughout the ecosystem.

STYLING

By relying upon partners for non-core functions, CE companies can focus on differentiators, such as styling. Product design is critical to creating a successful device. Thanks to smooth playlist control and seamless integration with download and management of songs, Apple has stormed the hallmarks of CE with its iPod. It is software that defines most of the "inner values" of consumer electronics. But as we know from social behaviorism, these values are primarily good for keeping an established relationship. To raise the first interest is what counts most. And again, Apple was able to find the right formula to make electronics irresistible even for people who don't care about technology.

Even in the 19th century, Anselm Feuerbach (German painter, 1828–1880) recognized that "style is knowing what to leave out." Some 150 years later, most CE executives still do not know. It takes a lot of management commitment to bring an unostentatious product to market. Ill-advised features and numerous buttons

---

15. "Videocon buys Thomson tube arm for Rs 1,272 cr," *The Financial Times Indian Express,* June 29, 2005.

could creep into the design if the technical engineer makes those decisions alone.

What really drives innovation that matters to the consumer in electronics, is simplicity. As renowned Jazz artist Charles Mingus said, "Making the simple complicated is commonplace; making the complicated simple, awesomely simple, that's creativity." Anybody can put out a technologically advanced product that is complicated, but an awesomely simple iPod-esque product really stands apart.

IT'S ABOUT SOFTWARE

Another differentiator in the CE industry is software. Most CE companies already employ more software than hardware engineers. Software makes the product more flexible. Just download a new application on the screen-equipped mobile communication device, and it morphs from a phone to a navigator to a telehealth-care hub. But software also makes the product more error-prone. Often simply downloading a new application causes a system shutdown. Companies that do their own software development—as well as those that have outsourced it—need to prudently design their requirements and quality management processes.

GLOBAL TECHNOLOGY OUTLOOK

Ultimately, it is the company with the best idea about the impact of future technology that gains the most from developments such as computing power leaps or compelling Smart Home applications. But one does not gain this understanding by looking through a crystal ball. Nor does the traditional approach of occasionally consulting the "company guru" deliver useful and timely information for making strategic decisions. In the emerging CE industry, the solid baseline for strategic company decision making is built by regular processes to evaluate the options using preset metrics and culminate in clear recommendations (see Chapter 8, "IBM's

Global Technology Outlook and Its Implications to Consumer Electronics" for more detail).

MARKETS BY GEOGRAPHY: CAPTURING THE BRICS

The BRIC countries are now entering their third phase of growth and innovation in CE. First, these countries were recognized as low-cost sources of labor and materials, which helped drive down costs and fuel rapid growth in Western markets. Second, the traditional global CE players saw the growth opportunity of these massive populations of potential electronics consumers. Now, the BRIC countries represent a new source of market growth and innovation by exporting their own products and becoming global industry players.

Unless a CE company has reliable sales data, it will probably have few ideas about consumer expectations in the fast-rising markets like Brazil, Russia, India, and China (the BRIC economies, as Goldman Sachs calls them).[16] Taking a closer look, as we did for China (see Chapter 13, "Consumer Electronics in China in Year 2011," for more detail), can provide exciting insight to what chances established CE companies of North America, Europe, Japan, and South Korea have in these geographies.

For example, phasing out old CRT monitors and focusing on the higher margin flat screens makes sense if that decision is based soundly on the company's strategy. However, one should not forget that there is a huge market for low-price, robust CRTs in countries like Brazil. Those CE companies that can leverage low-cost, written-off production lines, and optimize supply chains might be able to capture abandoned profits.

Especially for China, the picture becomes even more distinct. While a consumer also picks a standard Nokia mobile phone and thus buys the same products that appeal to Westerners, specialized

---

16. Wilson, Dominic and Roopa Purushothaman. "Dreaming With BRICs: The Path to 2050," Goldman Sachs Global Economics Paper No: 99, October 1, 2003.

versions of devices can be a big hit. Chinese companies that understand the incredibly huge domestic market have become powerful enough to start taking over firms and markets of the West. But their experience makes it apparent for all other companies that the CE industry will continue to be vividly shaken around.

CONCLUSION

The three M's—meta-value, models, and markets—will remain critical elements contributing to CE growth and innovation. As we continue to see the emergence of new technologies like Linux and the Cell processor being applied in the CE industry, we will naturally see the evolution of how services are provided and how business gets done. We will see intense focus on product design and developing innovative solutions that matter to consumers. We will see medical devices bringing the convergence trend to a far more personal and beneficial level, while games continue to keep us entertained with graphics and animation that are virtually indistinguishable from real life. We will see the increasing globalization of the emerging BRIC companies rock the industry as we know it today. We expect a great industry consolidation as those moving toward becoming On Demand Businesses adapt and respond to the new environment and emerge as industry leaders—the others will likely be consumed.

Whatever happens, people will still feel that urge to check out new technologies and gadgets. They still won't be able to help but imagine for a moment how a new device could somehow make their lives better, richer, or more complete. That is why electronics will continue to be irresistible.

2

The New Role of Technology and Services in Next-Generation Businesses

Nancy M. Forbes

Turbulence is perhaps the best overall one-word description of the environment in the world right now. History is unfolding daily as we experience geopolitical instability, a volatile state of the global economy, nuclear proliferation, dangerous new diseases, and declining trust in corporations and governments. The explanation for such turbulence and confusion is primarily twofold: (1) We have transitioned from an industrial, nation-based, resource-oriented economy to a networked, knowledge-intensive economy; and (2) The global market has become a reality, and the result is a realization of the complexity and complications of our world. Consumer electronics are the tangible assets that are present in each and every part of these economies and markets. Traditional approaches and mindsets will require rethinking to be successful in these new times. Or, as Edwill Jansen, IBM Electronics Executive puts it: "Electronics companies have enabled the world to become globalized, now these same companies are forced to redefine their position in the value network to survive because of globalization."

FOUR SIGNIFICANT TRENDS

Futurist Magazine has identified four significant trends (Universal Connectivity, Economic Globalization, Transactional Transparency, and Social Adaptation),[1] which have been adopted in this chapter to summarize driving changes in the marketplace. Prior to thinking through what impact these trends have on the future of business, it is first necessary to understand the significance of each trend.

It is important to keep in mind that every trend is impacted by countertrends that affect the timing and acceleration of the original trend.

While technology acceleration will offer many new possibilities, there will also be pushback, as society and individuals become more anxious about the consequences of change.

While the four primary trends themselves trigger change and yield questions coupled with potential opportunities, they also combine to drive marketplace shifts that will impact each and every business in a different way. Two marketplace shifts in particular will be most pertinent to a global electronics company given their posture on connectivity and globalization—the shift to Informed Interacting and the shift to a Next Generation Business Model. While these shifts are on the horizon, they are sure to accelerate over the next three to four years, so it is important to be thinking about them now to be prepared when the shifts become part of the mainstream.

TREND ONE: UNIVERSAL CONNECTIVITY

While information technology has provided many miraculous capabilities, it has given us only one new power that appears to have had significant impact on our collective behavior: our improved ability to communicate with each other anywhere, anytime.

Behavior researchers attribute mobile phones to having blurred or changed the boundaries between personal and public life. Most recently, instant messaging via mobile phones and PCs has begun

---

1.   Snyder, David P., "Five Meta-Trends Changing the World," *The Futurist*, July/August, 2004, p. 23.

to have an even more powerful social impact. Instant messaging provides a physical reality to cyberspace. It adds a new dimension to life given that communicators can now be *near, distant, or in cyberspace*.[2] When video instant messaging becomes more widely available in about three years, "the death of distance" will have been achieved.

Universal connectivity will be accelerated by the integration of the telephone, mobile phone, and other wireless telecom media with the Internet. By 2010, it is estimated that 80-90% of all Internet access will be made from Web-enabled phones, PDAs, and wireless laptops.[3] Thus, the Internet becomes the *infostructure* for the computer age. It has already largely contributed to speeding distributed workforces, reducing business travel volume, enabling outsourcing and global sourcing, as well as remote collaboration throughout supply chains. By 2010, we will be living "the global village," and cyberspace will be "the town square."[4] Yet the need for the tight-knit and much-missed community feel of traditional villages will never disappear, thus *nethoods*[5] will become more prevalent and mirror the addresses of the brick and mortar world.

UNIVERSAL CONNECTIVITY IN ACTION

TRENDWATCHING.COM, an independent consumer trend agency, coins ONLINE OXYGEN as a key trend stating that the online revolution has only just begun. "Eight years after the first Web sites started popping up, and email made its way from science labs to office desks and living rooms, 934 million consumers worldwide are beginning to see online access as an absolute necessity, comparable to oxygen, and there are no signs that the pace of integrating online access into daily life is slowing down. Being in control and communicating whenever/however is just too tempting."

---

2. Ibid.
3. Snyder, David P., "Five Meta-Trends Changing the World," *The Futurist*, July/August, 2004, p. 25.
4. Ibid.
5. "NETHOODS – An Emerging Consumer Trend and Related New Business Ideas," *Trendwatching.com*, August, 2004.

One of the biggest impediments to universal connectivity and the technological future is battery life. Even after a decade of impressive innovation in battery and "green" chip technologies, it becomes more apparent that Moore's law of a linearly increasing chip complexity over time could come to an ironic end—not because we can't build the next generation of chips, but because we can't power them. What is required is a pact made by the whole electronics industry (semiconductor equipment manufacturers, chipmakers, telecomm firms, battery companies, academia, and federal government) towards an electronic *Moore's Second Law*. The law would drive significant advancement even with a starting point such as:

Overall net efficiency of any electronic system will double every 24 months.

LOOKING AT MOORE'S LAW

In the April 19, 1965, edition of *Electronics*, Gordon Moore, then R&D director at Fairchild Semiconductor, first penned his now (in)famous "law" that the number of components on an integrated circuit would double every year. About 10 years later, he would revise that to a doubling every two years, and sometime later another Intel employee reinterpreted "Moore's Law" into its populist form that computing power would double every 18 months. The computer industry has driven to (and has been driven by) this trend very consistently across the intervening 40 years. Although today we may actually be seeing the performance trend suddenly slowing as power problems begin to overwhelm all other concerns.

One of the opportunities with the emerging personal and networked media is that it allows people to extend and express their identities, reputations, and personal passions in new ways among groups. This is exemplified in the success of open source where individual contributors participate in program solving in part because of their personal passions. Through their involvement, they also develop a reputation among the group, which is another type of motivation. A similar thing happens in the gaming environments. Creating these kinds of environments are really about *building social contexts* rather than *building technical systems*. For companies looking to stimulate innovation, it may be worth considering social platforms to benefit from the social interaction they enable. Consider for example *Eli Lilly's Innocentive,*[6] which acts as a portal for creating incentives for innovation. Innocentive has built a virtual community of 7000 single organic chemists with 2400 project rooms in use, organized around 33 problems.

TREND TWO: ECONOMIC GLOBALIZATION

Globalization theoretically has the potential to raise living standards and reduce the costs of goods and services for people everywhere. But the short-term marketplace consequences threaten many in both developed and developing nations. As a result, much of the focus on the global sourcing debate is on job loss and thus misses the many benefits of globalization that enable and energize innovative companies to tap the world's possibilities:

- **Reduced Costs.** Companies save (mainly in wages) on expenditures for business services that are globally sourced, thus enabling them to free resources to innovate and invest in activities that result in more added value opportunities.

- **New Revenue Markets.** Developing countries that provide offshore services need goods and services and so buy other things from developed country sources.

- **Redeployed Labor.** As was the case with manufacturing jobs being globally sourced over the past two decades, workers retrain for new jobs, which on the average pay more than the ones they replaced.[7]

---

6. www.innocentive.com.
7. Agrawal, Vivek, Farrell, Diana, "Who Wins in Offshoring," *The McKinsey Quarterly,* Number 4, 2003.

Over time, in industry after industry, a globalization story plays out necessitating shifts in the way we live and do business (Figure 2.1).

Figure 2.1   The globalization story.

This next economic phase will impact every part of living, from the kinds of work performed to the way citizens are educated and workers are trained. Most educational systems prepare children to live and work in a commodity driven economy where creativity and innovation might be considered liabilities. In the creative talent-based economy, invention and innovation will be paragon skills. Universal connectivity will also enable creative talent to be anywhere, forcing entities to have to figure out how to speak to, how to attract, and how to retain their share of the star talent that comes from all around the world.

TREND THREE: TRANSACTIONAL TRANSPARENCY

Fueled by the Internet and wireless technologies, the age of transparency will transform the way we live and work. Individuals, employees, business partners, customers, suppliers, shareholders, and local and global communities have unprecedented access and power to know what companies are up to. Whether it is employee abuse, the poor quality of a service or product, or hiding data from suppliers or stockholders, information on a transgression has the potential of getting out via the Internet and coming back to haunt the exposed company. Coupled with growing consumer vigilance, companies need to be prepared for retaliation from constituents who will eventually determine their fate. *Transactional transparency* exposes companies to their environment, rendering them essentially naked.

On the opening day of the movie, *The Hulk*, anticipated to be a Spider-Man-like blockbuster, bored viewers in the theaters began SMSing their peers outside to let them know that the movie was a dud even before it ended. They provided feedback to fellow potential product users around the world in the middle of the initial product experience. Compare this immediacy and power to previously available alternatives such as walking out or posting a review in the underground press—or even going online.[8]

In this environment, it is imperative to keep the confidence of all stakeholders with honesty, accountability, consideration, and transparency. What this means for each constituency is shown in the following list:

- **Employees.** Whether a company intends to or not, it leads by example. When employees do not trust a company, they won't build trust for that company with customers and business partners. Unethical employees have the potential for significant damage in a transparent environment.
- **Business Partners.** In the competition among supply chains, trust means lower costs and better performance. Sensing and tracking technologies will drive more accurate real-time information sharing.
- **Customers.** Transparency for customers can be a competitive differentiator either way. At one extreme, if a company does not have great products and fair prices, everyone will know instantly. At the other extreme, by sharing information such as source code with customers, the company builds a community of customer/developers and has gained, essentially for free, new markets, new product ideas, and street credibility.

---

8.   Gumbel, Andrew, "Texting blamed for summer movie flops," *The Independent,* August 18, 2003.

- **Communities.** This takes on two forms—philanthropy and accountability. The need for corporate philanthropy is obvious. On the subject of accountability, workers and business partners of companies belong to their own personal and professional "communities" whether local or not. Accountability for corporate responsibility and honest, open communications build community relationships.

- **Shareholders.** Owners of a company, its shareholders if public, have a right to know information about the company whether it's good or bad. Few companies of the Fortune 500, for example, report operating costs on a monthly basis, even though they could. Those that do, leverage transparency to build trust with shareholders.

Global governance is further challenged by corruption in governments throughout the world. Transparency International is a global organization that builds anticorruption coalitions with governments, business people, and civil society representatives such as The World Bank and the International Monetary Fund. They publish two annual reports that put pressure on governments tolerating high levels of corruption, and this spotlight has helped to raise public awareness of the issue. The Transparency International Corruption Perceptions Index charts levels of corruption in 145 countries (Table 2.1). In 2004, seven out of ten countries scored less than 5 out of a clean score of 10, while five out of ten developing countries scored less than 3 out of 10. This is concerning when you think of how transparent and global our world is becoming.

The Internet's transparency can also represent an extremely valuable form of social capital. What some companies have done is figured out how to leverage the transactional transparency of millions of people who trade or collaborate on their site into social capital and convert it into profits.

For example, one source of eBay's social capital is its feedback system, whereby buyers and sellers can rate each other. People need such confidence-building mechanisms to buy items from faceless strangers. Negative feedback is posted very rarely (less than 1% of the time), but sellers are afraid of getting any negative comments and go to great lengths to avoid them so their sales are not reduced.

Table 2.1   The Transparency International Corruption Perceptions Index 2004[9]

Country Rank	Country	2004 CPI Score*
1	Finland	9.7
2	New Zealand	9.6
3	Denmark	9.5
	Iceland	9.5
5	Singapore	9.3
6	Sweden	9.2
7	Switzerland	9.1
8	Norway	8.9
9	Australia	8.8
10	Netherlands	8.7
11	United Kingdom	8.6
12	Canada	8.5
15	Germany	8.2
17	USA	7.5
24	Japan	6.9
42	Italy	4.8
59	Brazil	3.9
71	China	3.4
90	India	2.8
	Russia	2.8
108	Argentina	2.5
145	Haiti	1.5

Note: Top 10 list, other countries of interest, and last.

Like other kinds of capital, social capital earns a return. One of the unique ways it pays off at eBay is in the thousands of small pricing and product selection innovations its members make to keep eBay's merchandising always in tune with the whims of the economy. No one single company could react as quickly as the millions of eBay users. MIT economist Erik Brynjolfsson describes it as "if you had a central purchasing department; you would not have all the creativity that the millions of people have who post on eBay

9.   Kotalik, Jana et al. (eds.), "Transparency International Annual Report 2004," Transparency International, Berlin, Germany, 2004.

trying to meet the unmet needs and develop products that might otherwise have gone unnoticed."[10]

TREND FOUR: SOCIAL ADAPTATION

Since the dawn of recorded history, societies have adapted to their changing circumstances. Cultural modernization has freed mature industrial nations from many societal restrictions of church and state, giving people much more freedom to be individually adaptive.

Many times, adaptive behavior is initially undertaken as a temporary measure, to be abandoned when circumstances return to normal. But the information revolution and the aging of mature industrial societies are not temporary, suggesting that at least some recent widespread innovations in lifestyle may be precursors of long-term or even permanent changes in society.

CHANGING DEMOGRAPHICS

Let's start with the information revolution. This revolution has created two segments that divide the population between *digital natives* (born roughly after 1980) and *digital immigrants* (born before 1980).[11] As shown in Table 2.2, digital natives have had an extraordinary, never-before-seen set of formative experiences based on the information revolution.

Contemporary neurobiology shows that experiences of this intensity alter the brains of those who take part in them in ways that enable the person(s) to accommodate and deal with these experiences more easily. So we now have a generation not only born into technology, but rewired in a way their parents never will be. This will affect how they operate in their lives and in the business world. No matter how fluent the digital immigrants become, they will always retain a digital immigrant accent, which can range from printing out emails to preferring to type with fingers versus

---

10. Schonfeld, Eric, "eBay's Secret Ingredient," *Business 2.0,* March, 2002.
11. Prensky, Marc, "The Death of Command and Control?," *Strategic News Service,* January, 2004.

thumbs. The digital native mindset is to use technology to effect immediate action.

Table 2.2   Lifetime Media Exposure of a 21 Year-Old Person

10,000 hours playing videogames

200,000 emails, instant messages sent/received

10,000 hours on mobile phones

20,000 hours watching TV

500,000 commercials seen

5,000 hours book reading

Digital Native Profile (people born roughly after 1980).[12]

Another aspect of the aging population means that companies have to gear up with products, services, and marketing targeted to aging consumers. Additionally it means that certain industries such as healthcare, real estate, financial services, insurance, entertainment, and so on might feel some significant rippling effect from this demographic shift. Business support organizations will have to determine where industry opportunities shift as a result of an aging population in developed countries worldwide.

ENVIRONMENTAL PROTECTION

Ecology is another area of social adaptation focus. If we want economic progress to continue, we must restructure the global economy to make it environmentally suitable. Today's global economy has been shaped by market forces, not by the principles of ecology. For example, clear-cutting a forest may be profitable for a logging firm, but it is economically costly to society as their natural support systems are being destroyed. Unfortunately, by failing to reflect the full costs of goods and services, the market provides misleading information to economic decision makers at all levels, thus creating a distorted economy.

---

12. Ibid.

Some countries are taking corrective actions. For example, the European Union has issued various regulations that put a focus on the environmental impact of consumer electronics:

- They prevent companies from using certain hazardous substances in consumer electronics products.[13]

- They require take back and encourage reuse of consumer electronics devices when these become waste.[14]

- They set a framework for how to design *Energy using Products* (EuP) with a constantly improved impact on the environment.[15]

WHAT THE TRENDS MEAN TO A CONSUMER ELECTRONICS COMPANY

In the last 24 months, the world has been pulled simultaneously by both the trends and their counter trends. The acceleration of these trends has been very aggressive, resulting in dilemma and tension as well as huge opportunities for those willing to change paradigms and mindsets. The integration of the trends drive shifts in the marketplace that will impact each and every business in different ways (Figure 2.2). Two marketplace shifts pertinent to a Consumer Electronics (CE) company are:

- FROM Transactional Computing TO Informed Interacting.

- FROM the Conventional TO the "Next Generation" Business Model.

---

13. ROHS - DIRECTIVE 2002/95/EC OF THE EUROPEAN PARLIAMENT AND OF THE COUNCIL of 27 January 2003 on the restriction of the use of certain hazardous substances in electrical and electronic equipment.
14. WEEE - DIRECTIVE 2002/96/EC OF THE EUROPEAN PARLIAMENT AND OF THE COUNCIL of 27 January 2003 on waste electrical and electronic equipment (WEEE).
15. EuP - DIRECTIVE 2005/32/EC OF THE EUROPEAN PARLIAMENT AND OF THE COUNCIL of 6 July 2005 establishing a framework for the setting of ecodesign requirements for Energy-Using Products [...].

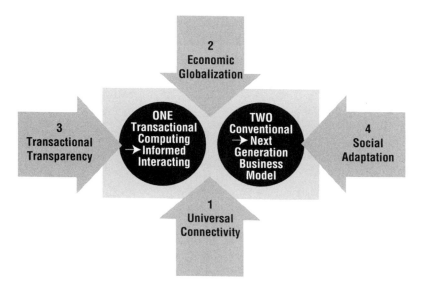

Figure 2.2   Trends and shifts pertinent to a CE company.

While just on the horizon now, these shifts are likely to accelerate over the next three to five years. So it is important to be thinking about them now in order to be prepared when the shifts become part of the mainstream.

MARKETPLACE SHIFT ONE: FROM TRANSACTIONAL COMPUTING TO INFORMED INTERACTING

Technologies rarely come along that impact collective behavior the way that the Internet has. The convenience of improved ability to communicate anywhere, anytime, on everything, coupled with a wealth of information access available, has enabled individuals to become more aware, sophisticated, and in control. This has driven an expectation for this convenient information-based experience to be the norm, to be pervasive in all aspects of life—personal, work, and as consumers.

The integration of the telephone, mobile phone, and other wireless telecom media with the Internet will further accelerate universal connectivity. By 2010, it is estimated that 80-90% of all Internet access will be made from Web-enabled phones, PDAs, and wireless laptops. Thus, the Internet will become the *infostructure* for the computer age. It has already largely contributed to speeding distributed workforces, reducing business travel volume, and enabling outsourcing and global sourcing, as well as remote collaboration throughout supply chains. This online revolution has only just begun.

Such universal connectivity has blurred the boundaries between work and social life and between personal and public life. That blurring also carries over to expectations of consumers and employees; for example, if they can communicate anytime and anywhere on everything, they expect to be able to do all of their activities (work and personal transactions) anytime, anywhere, on everything as well. The online oxygen has no boundaries, thus online control and communication are sought everywhere in life.

Universal connectivity also blurs the lines between computing, networking, and applications and requires a paradigm shift for computing from transacting to interacting. Businesses will need to start thinking about enabling transactions at the desired point of activity rather than from centralized system management points. Consider, for instance, the following scenario: A person is stuck in traffic and receives an instant message on his personal device with breaking news about a company in which he owns stock. He decides he wants to buy another thousand shares and would like to respond with an instant message containing an immediate purchase option, receive confirmation, and have all of his personal financial records updated while waiting in traffic. Why should that person have to go to a specific Web site to perform the transaction—or worse yet, have to call and conform to customer service menus and passwords? Why should this not be a flag to a finance company to update his financial records? Customers expect to be able to interact and conduct business anywhere, anytime, on everything as an extension of their accustomed lifestyle.

The immediacy of the information is as important as the immediacy to execute anytime and anywhere. It is the just-in-time information in the context of decision making that derives win-win value to both the user and provider of the information. In the stock purchase scenario, it was the fact that the person received timely and informative breaking news that triggered his desire to want to interact immediately—it could be a win-win in value for both the person stuck in traffic as well as the financial services firm pushing the information. Ironically, in this world of information overload, there is still a growing desire for actionable information. In fact, the added value of useful information is what ultimately grows a relationship between the business and customer and thus ultimately results in more revenue for business.

MARKETPLACE SHIFT TWO: FROM THE CONVENTIONAL TO THE "NEXT GENERATION" BUSINESS MODEL

The conventional hierarchal management and governance structure that was well suited for the industrial age has less relevance when applied to the majority of businesses that dominate the marketplace today. The success of today's businesses is a function of intangibles such as brand, employee knowledge, and the organizational capabilities of the firm to innovate. The basis of wealth creation has changed from capital to knowledge and from hard assets (plants, equipment, facilities) to soft ones (intellectual property, software code, processes, and relationships). The conventional business model has not kept pace with the transition from an industrial to a knowledge economy, leaving businesses ineffective in accommodating the shifting needs of business structure, human capital management, and governance.

THE IMPACT ON BUSINESS STRUCTURE

The hierarchical organization charts that have defined corporate life since the Industrial Revolution need to be redrawn. Back when business was more predictable and stable, companies organized themselves in vertical structures to take advantage of specialized experts. The benefits were obvious: clarity and stability. But the vertical alignment made it difficult for anyone to understand the task of the company as a whole and how it related to his/her work. To solve this problem, companies turned to matrix organizations, which essentially kept the hierarchy intact but facilitated the execution on projects that cut across departmental lines.

Organizations have become matrixed to an ineffective degree. Heightened globalization and increasing universal connectivity have led to employees, customers, suppliers, and partners of businesses being widely distributed, surfacing the need for more horizontally oriented communications and operations. Thus, corporate planners are starting to seek new solutions to accommodate the flatter "next generation" business that has evolved.

While the trend to flatter organizations has been underway for some time under the guises of total quality management, reengineering, business-process redesign, and matrix management, the "next generation" business structure would go much further than these previous efforts, basically eliminating both hierarchy and functional/departmental boundaries. While a skeleton group of senior executives may remain at the top in traditional support functions such as finance and human resources, everyone else in the organization would work together in multidisciplinary teams that perform processes centered on customers. Self-managing teams would become the building blocks of the new organization, and performance objectives would be linked to customer satisfaction rather than profitability or shareholder value.

The General Electric Company's $3 billion lighting business scratched a more traditional structure for its global technology organization in favor of one in which a senior team of nine to 12 people oversees nearly 100 processes or programs worldwide, from new-product design to improving the yield on production machinery. In virtually all the cases, a multidisciplinary team works together to achieve the goals of the process. The senior leadership group—composed of managers with "multiple competencies" rather than narrow specialists—exists to allocate resources and ensure coordination of the processes and programs. The change forced major upheavals in GE's training, appraisal, and compensation systems. To create greater allegiance to a process, rather than a boss, the company has begun to put into place so-called *360-degree appraisal routines* in which peers and others above and below the employee evaluate the performance of an individual in a process. In some cases, as many as 20 people are now involved in reviewing a single employee. Employees are paid on the basis of the skills they develop rather than merely the individual work they perform.

THE IMPACT ON HUMAN CAPITAL MANAGEMENT

In today's economy, the source of economic wealth is employees' creativity, knowledge, and passion. It has changed from capital to knowledge and from hard assets to soft ones. The future success of every business will depend on how well companies attract, motivate, and manage knowledge workers.

Add to this equation that knowledge workers are inherently unmanageable. Some interesting work has been done in this area by Next Generation Consulting, Inc. It is often the nature of both the individual and the job to figure things out for one's self. Couple this with the fact that those who have grown up in the information revolution, the digital natives, have a very different talent and attitude base thus causing their behaviour to be very different. Their attitudes toward authority are much more questioning and impatient as they are willing to accept responsibility to make a difference immediately. They are at ease in pointing out what they want and don't want. They have a strong preference for individuality, self-statement, and reluctance to conform to organizational or institutional directives or norms. And they are not motivated primarily by money but more so by the respect of their peers, challenge, and stimulation.

These trends indicate the need for a shift from a lean and mean people management approach to one that achieves breakthrough bottom-line performance because of people-centered policies that keep talented personnel engaged, committed, and loyal.

CONCLUSION

An understanding of the trends we laid out in this chapter explain why businesses are feeling frustrated by constant change—unpredictability and marginal growth. The resulting environment also demonstrates how the conventional hierarchal management and governance model that was well suited for the industrial age has less relevance when applied to the majority of businesses that dominate the marketplace today. The success of today's businesses is a function of intangibles such as brand, employee knowledge, and the organizational capabilities of the firm to innovate. Employees, customers, suppliers, and partners of businesses are continuously becoming more distributed across the globe. This has led to a growing need for more horizontally oriented communications and executions.

Companies that operate in the stormy environment of consumer electronics are most impacted by the new role of technology and services in next generation businesses.

After this broad perspective, you should be well suited to dive into the concrete issues, best practices, and challenges CE companies are facing.

3

The Consumer's Internet— Thin Clients & Fat Hosts for Everyone

Stephen J. Andriole,
Charles B. Whinney, IV

The World Wide Web is all-inclusive. There's not much one cannot find, analyze, or purchase on the Web. The past ten years has seen the evolution of the Web from a passive repository of information to a proactive pusher of content and a ubiquitous enabler of transactions. Educational curricula, music, films, surveys, customer service portals, travel planning, job placement boards, and even personal matchmaking services are all on the Web. For some, the Web is woven so deeply into the fabric of their lives that it's impossible for them to imagine a disconnected world.

This chapter suggests that the best way for consumers to exploit the Web is through the thinnest of clients, devices that are extremely cheap, durable, and easy to use. Conversely, we argue here that the worst way to exploit the emerging Web is to design and field large, complex, expensive access devices designed to do everything one might imagine on or offline, devices that will be hard to configure, optimize, and support, and because of their cost and complexity, actually stifle the growth of the Web as a consumer portal. This is all illustrated early on in the chapter with a scenario that describes how the world will work in the early 21st century.

THE LONG ARM OF THE WEB

Business-to-business (B2B) commerce is now part of how companies save and make money, and while we're all pretty comfortable with buying books, CDs, and DVDs from www.amazon.com, we've only just begun to integrate the Web's contents and capabilities into our personal lives. Here's a short list of just how personal it's all getting:

- Buy and sell all varieties of stuff including clothes, employees, services, and so forth.
- Negotiate and partner with each other and each other's digital assistants.
- Advertise and market goods, services, likes, and dislikes.
- Manufacture all sorts of things including ideas.
- Distribute the things we make, think, share, and negotiate.
- Communicate online or offline with friends, families, lovers, employees, and so on.
- Entertain ourselves, our friends, our kids, and our enemies.
- Heal the routinely ill, the desperately ill, and the neurotically ill.
- Govern our school boards, associations, and governments.
- Learn what we want to learn and need to learn whenever we like.

The interesting thing about the Web is that everyone understands it in pieces. Teenagers think the Internet is after-school Instant Messaging and MP3 downloads. Researchers think the Internet is an endless source of "linked" information. Those who've purchased a book or CD online think the Internet offers great selections and a way to save time. Entrepreneurs still think the Internet is a gold rush, and established businesses without cool Web sites think the Internet is a threat to profitability. The amazing thing about all this is that while everyone is right, everyone's also missing the point: Taken together, all of these pieces—and lots more—represent the most profound change any of us have ever experienced, studied, or even imagined.

Internet usage has increased at a rate faster than television, the VCR, radio, air travel, automobile travel, and CDs. Consider that the Internet represents the near reversal of personal and commercial transaction power. For the first time in history, communicators, negotiators, buyers, and sellers are all on a level playing field. Also, the Internet is viral. It expands exponentially as the number of Internet users grows. It's also the world's first personal medium. We're on the verge of mass personalization where Web sites will greet, recognize, and cater to all of us as individuals with specific needs and desires. When was the last time your television wished you happy birthday and suggested a present you might ask someone to buy for you? Finally, the Internet is instantly global in that a Web site can be accessed by anyone, at anytime, from anyplace.

But all of this represents the tip of the iceberg, as the following scenario describes.

HOW THE WORLD WILL WORK

It's February 13, 2015 …

Characters:

> **Thomas Everyperson**—you, me, anyone, and everyone
>
> **Katherine Everyperson**—same
>
> **Randolph**—the ubiquitous digital concierge
>
> **The House**—very, very smart

Thomas and Katherine are awakened by a digital clock with a light pulse at 6AM, followed by Randolph's greeting.

Randolph: "Are we awake? Here's the deal (Randolph has just the right personality). Katherine, you have three appointments this morning and two this afternoon. You also have a four o'clock meeting with the builder (they're building a new car). Thomas, your day is free. Would you like some suggestions about what you might do?"

Thomas: "Sure, what do you have in mind?"

Randolph: "With your permission, we could complete the financial review we started last month, scout the trip to Cabo, or visit the colleges you might want Emily (their daughter) to visit. And you both have to vote on the tax referendum before midnight. We could also train. You're behind in your weight loss plan."

Thomas: "And you're a pain in my derriere."

Randolph: "Relatively small pain, sir, given the current size of your derriere."

Katherine: "I love it. Randolph is a mind reader! Who programmed him, anyway? Can we do the design meeting remotely? I'd prefer to do it from here."

Randolph: "I'll arrange it."

While Thomas and Katherine shower and dress, their activities are monitored. When they leave their dressing areas and arrive in the kitchen, the coffee is hot and Katherine's oatmeal is prepared. The house has come alive. Sixty minutes before Thomas and Katherine rose, the heat was increased, the blinds and curtains were raised, and the latest news was scanned and presented for review (Katherine still prefers to read "the paper," so Randolph has it printed, while Thomas prefers to read his news directly from the wireless screen that he carries around with him all over the house or the permanent screens embedded in more than a few walls).

All communications are wireless. Information pours in from several approved sources. The house is endowed with sensors in just about everything. Lights know what time it is, the refrigerator knows what's almost gone (and then reorders it), and their clothes know when they're dirty. The house plants ask for water when they're dry, and each room plays the right music at the right time.

Randolph is the ultimate impresario. He has learned all about the Everypersons and gets smarter each day. He is in fact a computer program—based on a neural network (a simulated human brain)—that can understand conversational and formal speech and speak in whatever language (and tone) Katherine and Thomas prefer. He is so smart that he even knows what he doesn't know but knows where to find whatever information he needs.

Randolph is also part of a confederation of intelligent concierges that meet and work in cyberspace. They wheel and deal, argue and transact 24 hours a day. In fact, Randolph himself has digital kids that he dispatches over the World Wide Web to do all kinds of things on his behalf. When Katherine and Thomas want to travel to Europe, the kids hit the Web for deals (but when it comes time to actually booking the deal, Randolph negotiates the price).

Everything now has an Internet "address". That means cars, clothes, appliances, walls, and air conditioners—just to name a few of the more obvious things. All have identities, conditions, and sense → think → act capabilities—and they all communicate with one another, so when the house is hot and the shades are open, the heat will go down and the shades will close—and a query will be launched to determine how the house got that way in the first place.

No one actually pays bills. Instead, once a month everyone gets a statement of activity that lists all of the transactions executed on their behalf—and that Randolph manages. If there are any irregularities, Randolph will handle them—unless he gets in over his head or if the regularities exceed his assigned authority. When he gets confused, he'll first ask his confederates for help and then Katherine and Thomas—but only when he's desperate.

The world in 2015 is light years from where it was when we all worried about routine tasks—and sweated out the details of life's major events. Information is abundant and the thought of doing "research" as everyone once did it is foreign to 21st century kids, adults, and scholars. The new problem is information overload, but "infomediaries" and other filters are widely available, very smart, and very amenable to individual desires. Randolph, for example, stands between the world of information and problem-solving: if you need it, Randolph gets it for you, but if you don't, you never see it.

No one buys commodities at malls anymore. Malls have become mega entertainment centres where people go to socialize and be entertained. Commodities are purchased automatically and seamlessly. Randolph and his associates execute just about all commodity transactions. No one personally goes to a Web site to buy a book or CD; Randolph takes care of all that, buying the commodity from whoever will sell it the cheapest and get it to you the fastest. In fact, by 2015, the number of Web pages has actually declined dramatically from its height in 2005.

The world has physically and virtually converged. We no longer have computers, mobile phones, personal digital assistants, or pagers. We have single devices that do multiple things. We no longer distinguish between streaming video and television.

Content-on-demand has changed the way we think, learn, live, and love. And the content is immersible. Through virtual reality tours, we are able to experience all sorts of things (before we buy), including cars and vacations.

4PM

Randolph: "Katherine, can you take the meeting with the architect for your car? And how would you like to immerse yourself?"

Katherine: "Give me five minutes and then connect me here (Randolph knows where she is). I'd like to fully immerse myself this time. Thanks."

5 Minutes Later

Randolph: "I'm connecting Katherine, Charlie (the architect), and 'Katrina' (the car). Katherine, you can start whenever you want." (Katherine accesses the virtual car and test track.)

Katherine: "This feels terrific. What did you do?"

Charlie: "I raised the windshield three inches and lowered the steering wheel to give you a better feel for the road. Given your height and weight, I figured it would improve the driving experience."

Katherine (Still driving): "You were right. Thanks." (Custom cars? Mass customization will be the rule, and individuals will be able to drive, fly, taste, and feel virtual prototypes just about anytime they want.)

6PM

Randolph: "I need both of you before midnight and preferably now. We've got to register our vote about the proposed tax increase. I've already given you the details and the recommendation—given your financial goals. Are you still confident voting against the referendum?"

Thomas: "Yes. Do it."

Katherine (Still driving): "Yes, yes, yes. I need all the money I can get to pay for this car . . . "

Randolph (Privately to Thomas): "Thomas, I've ordered a dozen roses for Katherine and placed a gift certificate for some virtual tours in her mailbox. She gets to pick her favourite real thing—up to $3,000. OK?"

Thomas: "No. What's the hell's going on?"

Randolph: "Valentine's Day, Thomas . . . "

Randolph (Privately to Katherine): "What would you like me to arrange for Valentine's Day?"

Katherine: "What do you have in mind?"

Randolph: "How about some virtual tours that Thomas can select from? I think he'd like that."

Katherine: "Perfect. Thanks."

Katherine and Thomas will select the same experience. Randolph has arranged for the couple to think they're perfectly simpatico.

THIN IS GOOD

About 10 years ago, Larry Ellison appeared on the Oprah Winfrey Show to discuss "network computers". This was when many great-but-ahead-of-their-time ideas were out there, like Apple's Newton and IBM's voice recognition applications. Larry was wrong then because our networks weren't reliable, secure, or ubiquitous enough to support "thin client" architectures. Never mind that the devices themselves were form-factor-weird and way too propri-etary. But if Larry reprised his appearance on Oprah tomorrow, he'd be dead right.

This chapter takes Larry's "thin is good" argument to a new place. In fact, we'll argue here that the Internet is the ultimate virtual server and all that anyone needs to access its content and trans-action capabilities is a very thin, throw-away consumer client. The argument obviously is that we should focus much more on the vir-tual server than on the device used to access it. In fact, given communications technologies and trends, it makes sense to invest in the "host" much more than the "client". There's also the digital divide issue: The cheaper the access device, the more people can participate in the digital consumer revolution.

Let's look at several trends that point to why this approach makes sense.

First and foremost, network access is almost ubiquitous today: We use desktops, laptops, personal digital assistants (PDAs), thin clients, and a host of multi-functional converged devices, such as integrated pagers, mobile phones, and PDAs to access local area networks, wide area networks, virtual private networks, the Internet, and hosted applications on these networks, as well as applications that run locally on these devices. The networks work.

The cost to acquire, install, and support the devices, however, is out of control. The Gartner Group, for example, reports that the annual support cost for a single wireless PDA is nearly $4500 per employee, per year.

Small, cheap, reliable devices that rely on always-on consumer networks make sense. Shifting computing power from desktops and laptops to professionally managed servers makes sense.

Moving storage from local drives to remote storage area networks makes sense. Fat clients should lose some weight—as we bulk up our already able, under-utilized servers. The total-cost-of-owner-ship (TCO)—not to mention the return-on-investment (ROI)—of skinny client/fat server architectures is compelling.

IT'S ABOUT THE DEVICE

One way to approach this is to begin with what the ideal converged device might look like and then strip it down to make it as thin and cost-effective as possible—while still allowing it to be functional. Some characteristics of "fat clients" now deployed and that are under development include:

- Small (pocketable, about the size of a larger PDA on the market today) with as large a screen as possible within the given form factor.
- Touch-screen.
- Expandable memory.
- GSM or CDMA cellular phone service with broadband (EV-DO or EDGE).
- Address/phone book.
- MP3 playback (via broadband or memory).
- Video playback (via broadband or memory).
- Web browsing with full Java support.
- Popular OS allowing wide-range of programs (PalmOS or Win Mobile).
- Camera with video capabilities.
- GPS with full mapping capabilities.
- Bluetooth (file transfer, keyboard, headset, etc. compatibility).
- Wi-Fi.

The likely initial cost for such devices is in the $500–$700 range. Over time, we can certainly expect the costs to drop, but the on-going maintenance and replacement costs for such powerful devices will remain substantial.

What if there was another way to exploit all of that content and transaction processing capability? What if we could develop devices so thin and cheap that everyone could afford one? What might these devices look like? Here are some of the characteristics such devices might have:

- Even smaller form-factor (comfortably pocketable; about the size of a nonflip mobile phone), as large a screen as possible in that form-factor.

- Touch screen.

- GSM or CDMA mobile phone service with Internet, ideally with broadband.

- Web browsing with full Java (or any open standard) support that makes email client, word processor, audio/video playback, and so on available without installing applications, which can be accessed directly from the Web.

It's important to note that the technology is certainly already here for companies to make these devices in these form-factors, so long as they remain "open." Any Bluetooth phone currently offered by Verizon, for example, has reduced Bluetooth functionality and does not allow a user to transfer files. This allows the company to protect their business model, which requires people to pay for programs, ringers, wallpaper, and so on. One of the main reasons the iTunes mobile phone got delayed is because providers keep changing their minds on how they want to charge users for the songs, while still allowing Apple to get their percentage of the transactions. As the industry moves toward more open standards, many of these problems and incompatibilities will disappear.

Wide-area wireless network technologies, such as WiMAX, have the potential to drastically reduce the price of such devices. With WiMAX, companies could blanket entire cities with WiFi-like broadband Internet service. This would not only enhance the "always-on" nature of a device, but potentially could render the entire mobile phone industry obsolete due to VoIP services. Devices would only need the Internet.

We estimate that over time, the cost for ultra thin devices will be much less than $100. We would expect that these thin Web clients would literally become throw-aways, thus eliminating completely the break-and-fix/replacement cycle that plagues so many IT shops and frustrates so many not-so-technology-savvy consumers. The price point would also make the clients affordable to just about everyone.

IT'S ABOUT THE MODEL

There are several models here—the model of how the Web should work, the technology that powers it, and the business model that determines how people make money—the lifeblood of all consumer technology models.

First, let's acknowledge that the Internet has matured dramatically over the past decade. It is faster, more reliable, more secure, and more flexible than it was when it was essentially a large database server. It's now a ubiquitous platform on which all sorts of content sits. It has extended to retail outlets, malls, coffee shops, and other recreational areas. Several cities have announced plans to provide wireless access to the Web to their entire metropolitan regions; other cities will soon follow. Access to the Web has climbed dramatically in the past few years and in some countries access is approaching 100%.

A simple extrapolation indicates that within a few years, all of the industrialized nations will have near-100% access. The Internet is a passport to endless communications, content, and transactions. There's great appeal in stepping back from managing any aspect of the communications infrastructure or content management on fat devices that require their own substantial care and feeding. When the industry first started thinking about thin clients—even before Larry Ellison's appearance on Oprah Winfrey's show—everyone understood the network and transaction processing implications of thin client architecture. In those days, there was a lot of uncertainty about just how to power the transactions that a 24/7 network would deliver. But more recently, architectures have developed that suggest just how a thin client/fat host might work. New service oriented architectures (SOA) will make it possible for transaction power—and flexibility—to reside on distributed servers capable of communicating and fabricating transactions at a moment's notice. SOA combined with AJAX (asynchronous JavaScript and XML) will make it possible for consumers to use incredibly skinny devices to accomplish all sorts of Web-based activities. What this all means in practice is that our ability to extend distributed computing is growing dramatically and that new architectures will make it possible to imagine all sorts of seamless, instant (in addition to secure) communications from all sorts of devices—including ultra thin ones.

There's also the business model. How will people make money in a thin client/fat host world?

Needless to say, money will be made building the devices and super-charging the browsers necessary to exploit new SOA and AJAX capabilities. But most of the money will be made by the utility model suggested by thin client/fat host Web computing. Consumers will pay for what they use, as they use it; they will not pay for subscriptions or the equivalent of enterprise licenses that may or may not be used enough to justify the initial and on-going fees. The model suggested here is similar in concept to the utility computing model that many companies believe will define how technology is acquired and deployed in the near future. "Paying by the drink" is one of the mantras of the utility computing movement, a mantra that we believe will extend to the consumer market where's there's already lots of precedents for its acceptance and success.

The fat hosts will require no subscription fees. These hosts will primarily blanket services over one another, like enabling a consumer to watch his or her cable television feed on their thin device.[1] Fat hosts that provide services as such have the potential to revolutionize the cable and satellite TV industry. These companies will eventually abandon their existing distribution models in favor of distributing their services through the Internet.

The proliferation of wide area wireless networks will also force the mobile phone companies to alter their distribution models. With a

---

1. www.slingmedia.com.

technology such as WiMAX built into inexpensive thin clients, consumers will no longer need to be connected to anything besides the Internet as all other services become blanketed over it. If only one primary technology manifests itself, these companies will simply become wireless Internet service providers, each being a different means for users to connect to the exact same network.

CONCLUSION

Randolph would be happy in this world. Not only does he not have to worry about the care and feeding of a fat client clogged with bloatware (and viruses), but he is also comforted by the fact that just about everyone can participate in the ultimate consumer portal.

But just as there have been problems with the adoption of thin clients in the corporate world, we can expect obstacles here as well. Not technical obstacles but "political" ones, ones anchored in the inertia of how we've always done things, how many still believe computing power should be allocated.

Hopefully over time, opinions will evolve to include a role for thin Web clients—a role that everyone can play.

4

The Smart Home: Coming to Your House Soon, but Not Too Soon

Ralf Baral, Christian Schiller, Allan Henderson

A Smart Home is *not* a home that does calculus problems for fun, nor does it play chess with other homes in the neighbourhood.

A Smart Home is a digitally automated living environment (a house) that can make your life more convenient. A Smart Home can allow the different parts of a home or devices in a home to be controlled remotely. Or better yet, the Smart Home can automatically respond to persons living in it, as if they were living inside an automated robot-butler that is very attentive to their needs.

For example, you arrive home in the evening, and your house itself senses that you're there, setting the lights to your liking for evenings at this time of year, setting the temperature to your liking for the time of day and year, and turning on just the background music that you like after a day's work.

Smart Homes are houses wherein the home's digital devices are interconnected and talk to each other—and are under your control. A Smart Home integrates the digital control of your home's lighting, heating, security, entertainment (music, film, or TV), and even everyday home appliances (refrigerator, washing machine, microwave oven, and toaster).

And you control it all from your cell phone or small computer. The Smart Home collects and evaluates real-time data from the home's digital devices (for example, the operating conditions of the heating system) and either reacts in a predefined way or alerts you that you need to take some action.

If you look back over time, you'll notice that the typical household is following a slow but continuous evolution toward a Smart Home. Today, the average private household is more and more likely to have fast, broadband access line, a number of home applications with the potential for operational intelligence, and a familiarity with using the Internet. Homes are filled with digital devices driven by microprocessors. Homes are connected to the Internet with dial-up or broadband access and are connected to phone line, TV cable lines, and satellite TV and radio transmissions. So by 2004, already 37 million home networks had been installed.[1]

Analysts expect that the market for telecommunications providers to private households along with the sales of smart digital home devices and appliances will reach US $20 billion by 2009.[2]

HOW TO GET A SMART HOME TODAY

Bill Gates has been building a Smart Home, but he's the richest man in the world. Most of us don't have anywhere near the resources of Bill Gates.

Can the average consumer have a Smart Home today? The answer is technically yes because the technology elements exist, and the prices continue to fall as they continue to do for all consumer electronics products. However, there are other problems.

---

1. "Digital Domicile 2005: Wireless Overtakes Ethernet," *In-Stat*, July 2005.
2. Ibid.

To have a Smart Home, you really need just two affordable pieces of technology:

- A broadband communications infrastructure in the house that can connect digital devices together.
- High-function digital devices that can connect to the communications infrastructure and work together.

Most consumer products are controlled by digital processors, and communications infrastructures are becoming more and more common in many homes. Wireless networks already exist in many homes, connecting home computers to the Internet. And many other homes have cable TV lines, telephone lines, and satellite TV receivers. The problem is becoming one of too many communication infrastructures.

So the technology is here. The big questions are: Do enough people really want a Smart Home? And do they want one enough to create a consumer demand in the marketplace?

WHAT ARE THE BARRIERS FOR THE EMERGING MARKET OF SMART HOMES?

Four significant barriers exist for the emerging market of Smart Homes:

- Consumer's perception of value.
- Product and company readiness.
- Affordability for a mass market.
- Ecosystem needs.

PERCEPTION OF VALUE FOR CONSUMERS

Does the average person really need a Smart Home? Is convenience enough of a value driver to open the market beyond the early adopters and get it into the mass market?

The consumer is the best indicator for the value of a solution. But if you ask consumers today, they will tell you that the solution offerings for Smart Home do not yet provide enough real value.

There are a high number of model homes available in countries around the world. These model homes are positioned to be show rooms of a future way of living, places where companies demonstrate their power of innovation. Very few are offering a living environment where people like you and me would like to stay and enjoy this better future—such a good future that consumers would be willing to pay for this convenience as well as security, peace of mind, safety, and many other benefits. And there is no doubt that without a revenue stream coming from a consumer, not much will progress from this model home environment.

The Smart Home market would benefit most from a "killer application" that consumers just can't live without. Or perhaps it needs an "evolution path" where you can start with a few smart devices and keep adding until you find you have a complete Smart Home.

PRODUCT AND COMPANY READINESS

Many current consumer electronic devices can already be easily networked and are able to communicate and interoperate with other devices. Turning on the TV will dim the lights and turn off the radio—and perhaps even start the popcorn popping.

You will become accustomed to

- Devices designed to easily interoperate. Consumer electronics companies are already building devices that can talk to each other. But this is only a start before most of them are designed with interoperability as a standard feature.

- Immediately connecting the various devices to a network. It still is a hard task to make one device talk to another, even if they are designed with the capability to interconnect. There's a long way to go in making it easy for a new device to snap into an existing Smart Home network and immediately start talking to the other devices.

Some of the key issues here include simplicity of user interfaces, speech-enablement, and easy remote management.

However, the open question is this: How does the product look in the context of a Smart Home service environment? Maybe the idea of a "product" has to be replaced by a "service offering"? This might happen, but companies are short on solutions for it. The technology is available for CE companies to manufacture the devices needed for the Smart Home, and the telecommunications companies today have solutions available to bring the infrastructure.

But will the CE and telecommunications companies be able to generate enough demand to run a profitable business? It will all come down to the viability of the business models. It seems the most promising business model is one in which services play a big role. The lessons we learned over the last 10 years in dealing with Smart Homes is this: If the industry focuses on products instead of services and content, there will be no readiness for a Smart Home.

A utility like a gas or electric company is able to provide the product as a service based on an infrastructure called a distribution network that is pervasive in most parts of the developed world. This pre-investment came without a real business risk, while living in a regulated market in the past. Unfortunately, there is no low risk approach to the Smart Home infrastructure. A business needs to take all the risk of entering a brand new market, facing customers for the first time, and delivering a maximum level of service right from the start.

The Smart Home becomes a system, in which each part plays a role in relation to other parts. So some products need to play subordinate roles in the system—everyone can't be the star of the play. This is only viable in a very new ecosystem where companies cooperate and compete at the same time. However, so far, most companies are focusing only on competition, not on cooperation.

AFFORDABILITY AS MASS MARKET SOLUTION

A fully assembled Smart Home tends to be pricey. Few products run in a larger number of homes, so the owner has perhaps spent millions to enable and thousands per month to operate the house.

Take a simple example: When you switch on the television in a Smart Home, your room can automatically be set for television viewing—the lights are dimmed, and the radio switched off. There is no question this means convenience. But is it enough convenience for the price? The total cost of ownership (TCO) is still far too high and not equivalent to the value delivered.

The primary reason for this is that neither consumer electronics nor other household devices are designed for interoperability.

Companies protect their portfolio by providing integrated solutions based on proprietary standards that prohibit the combination company X's refrigerator with company Y's oven. Built-in interoperability would allow application companies to deliver smart and cheap applications, immediately integrating the home.

The best way to solve this problem is by broadly adopting open standards. When consumers demand cross-brand interoperability, the manufacturers will want to adhere to those open standards in their new products.

ECOSYSTEM NEEDS

A Smart Home needs a support infrastructure just like a car does. If gas stations and auto repair shops were not common, few people would have a car. Just as the gas stations and repair shops are part of the auto ecosystem, devices, services, infrastructure, and so forth need to be part of a Smart Home ecosystem.

In a new emerging market, new roles are needed to support the total life cycle of smart home products and business.

You can think of these phases of the lifecycle:

1. Development.
2. Marketing, sales, and installation.
3. Operation and maintenance.
4. Continuous adaptation.

Here we will focus on the current state of the Smart Home market—the development phase. The roles and skills required for this phase comprise the provision and connection of a Smart Home system to the mass market.

After acquiring the products and devices for a Smart Home, someone needs to establish the system and make sure it actually works. Usually the marketing and sales forces of CE product manufacturers focus on their own products. A Smart Home *system,* however, requires also a systems engineer with the following competencies:

■   Design a Smart Home systematically during the planning phase.

■   Do the installation and integration of the Smart Home solution.

■   Test the live workings of the Smart Home.

■   Do on-going maintenance for the Smart Home.

This system engineer will ensure that the complexity of integrating heterogeneous devices and solutions into one system and provide a single point of control for the consumer (Figure 4.1).

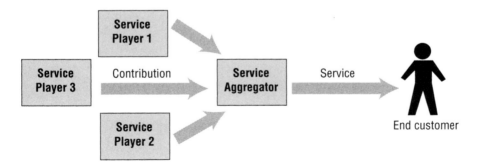

Figure 4.1   A new service model with competition and cooperation.

The system engineer will be required in all phases of the lifecycle of a Smart Home. Unfortunately, this skilled role is not available for mass market offering at an affordable price—yet. This is critical, especially as this profession is also the key to allow open systems to win over proprietary systems and therefore accelerate the introduction and acceptance of Smart Homes for the mass market.

But other roles, too, are missing for mass market readiness of Smart Homes:

- Where is the architect who can design/redesign a Smart Home?
- Where is the installer providing an integrated solution?
- Where is the company providing integration applications for homes?
- Where is the business broker defining the portfolio of services and marketing, selling, delivering, and maintaining this in a customer facing role?

A QUICK SUMMARY OF THE SMART HOME MARKET ENVIRONMENT (2005)

A joint team from Hannover University and Purdue University recently (2005) assessed the Smart Home Marketplace for IBM. This study shows that the progress of the Smart Home with focus on technologies is currently hindered by issues in three main areas: demand, technology standards, and incomplete knowledge of consumer wants and needs.

Table 4.1 summarizes many of the key findings from the study.

Smart Home technology is still evolving. Research is being performed by research groups in universities, computer-technology companies, electronics OEMs, and telecommunications companies.

Table 4.1 Smart Home Marketplace Study for IBM

Business (Demand)	Technical	Consumer
Lack of demand for remote-controlled appliances	Lack of reliability regarding voice recognition systems	Lack of research regarding how people use the spaces in which they live
Lack of extended demand for DSL, a telecom channel enabling efficient Smart Home technology[3]	Lack of practical experience regarding cable as a medium for video connection among persons	Lack of understanding regarding the specific needs of the (non-wheelchair-bound) disabled
	Difficult to passively monitor (e.g., with a wrist transmitter) vital functions of the elderly and disabled	
	Difficult to set up an integrated home-networking architecture such that one switch, meant for the end-user, wirelessly forms the appropriate controlling functions over a range of devices	
	Additional conflict of interest: ensuring the privacy of a home digital network while preventing its interference with other networks	

WHAT IF THERE ISN'T A "KILLER APPLICATION"?

We mentioned earlier that the market is still looking for the "killer application" to push the Smart Home market forward.

NOTE

The best chance for a "killer application" seems to be through telehealthcare, as discussed in Chapter 5, "Telehealthcare: The Key to the Living Room."

---

3. Berlo, Ad van, "Design Guidelines on Smart Homes A COST 219bis Guidebook," AFONSO Lonay, CH, Oct. 1999.

But we might realize that there is no killer application for the Smart Home. In that case, we have a couple of other options for moving the Smart Home forward in the market:

- Target the appeal of the Smart Home to the traditional early adopters of technical gadgets, the people who like technology for technology's sake. This is the traditional market for many electronics gizmos.

- Aim at a niche market where the perceived need is greatest, such as homes where the elderly or the sick need additional care. The house and its devices can help monitor the person living in it, and it can sound various levels of alarm if something out of the ordinary happens.

- Aim at high-end home construction firms that want to differentiate their homes from other high-end homes. The car industry took this approach with CD players and GPS devices for high-end models.

TECHNOLOGY SOLUTION ARCHITECTURE FOR SMART HOMES

A diverse ecosystem of service providers, content providers, and CE manufacturers—rallied together by a Smart Home Service Operator (SHSO)—is the key premise for successfully delivering convenient value-added Smart Home services to consumers as "one-stop shopping."

The technological impact of this new, unique business model is quite high because no existing "standard" e-business architecture pattern fits into the business model requirements.

Solutions for the Smart Home need to easily interoperate, which can best be achieved by adhering to open standards.

To give the technically interested reader the chance to dive a bit deeper into this area, which might become the single most important control point for consumer electronics, we have added the following architecture sections.

ARCHITECTURE OVERVIEW

Figure 4.2 shows a high-level architectural view of the Smart Home environment, from a technology standpoint.

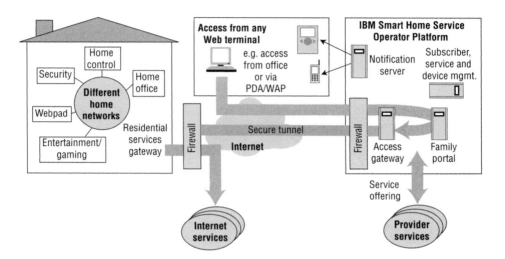

Figure 4.2   Architecture overview.

Local technologies and services are aggregated on the residential service gateway, which is the single entry point in the household from a communications point of view. Core of the gateway is the OSGi (an open cross-industry alliance) service platform that serves as the aggregation layer for technologies and services.

User interface integration is running on the residential gateway on the Application Layer, namely through an implementation of a Web-based embedded portal. Various clients, from a notebook to a handheld or TV, can be used for that via fixed or wireless networks.

Connectivity between the residential gateway and the Smart Home Service Operator platform (SHSO) is achieved by establishing a secure IP tunnel over wide area networks.

The service operator platform consists of the following main components, plus various other "infrastructure" components (such as databases, directory, application servers, and so on):

- Authentication, authorization, and virtual private network capabilities.
- Subscription Management—manages platform users and their subscribed services.
- Device Management—manages gateway device configuration.
- Portal Server—provides the family portal.
- Notification Services.

OPEN SERVICES GATEWAY INITIATIVE (OSGI)

The OSGi consortium was founded in 1999 with the objective to create open specifications for the network delivery of managed services to local networks and devices. It defines an open, common architecture for service providers, developers, software vendors, gateway operators, and equipment vendors to develop, deploy, and manage services in a coordinated fashion. Thus an entirely new category of "smart devices" with flexible and managed deployment of services can be created. OSGi is related to other Java standards such as Java 2 Micro Edition.

OSGi enables incremental platform upgrades and extensions in mission critical "always on" situations such as in a gateway. It enables the installation and running of disconnectable applications from multiple independent sources and viable management systems for resource constrained devices.

RESIDENTIAL SERVICE GATEWAY

A Residential Service Gateway (RSG) is an OSGi service platform that acts as a gateway between the in-house local area network(s) and a wide area network, such as the Internet. It integrates and abstracts the available home networks (for example Ethernet, wireless LAN, and home automation technologies) using OSGi services. It also provides for the integration of intelligent appliances and other services.

With the secured connection to the Internet, the residential service gateway becomes the central access point to a machine site— a car or a house. It can be a router, server, and firewall for other PCs on the network; the messaging gateway between different local networks, such as power line and entertainment networks; and the runtime environment for user interfaces and business logic.

Different devices will host functions of the gateway. In home environments, the gateway itself does not have to be a separate box. It can also be integrated into a Set-Top-Box, a television, or a mounted kitchen console. If home security functions are included a separate box, it should be placed in a secure environment.

SMART HOME SERVICE OPERATOR PLATFORM

The service operator platform comprises the necessary infrastructure to manage and deliver Smart Home services from a Smart Home services operator standpoint, taking into account that an OSGi-based residential service gateway is part of the Smart Home service delivery.

Complex systems can be viewed both from a functional and an infrastructural standpoint. The functions this platform provides are an environment for service creation (IP-Store, which includes Smart Home Service provisioning), the device and software management for the residential service gateway, as well as the actual delivery of Smart Home services.

To provide these functionalities, a component might need to use or include several infrastructure components, such as data stores, runtime environments, or components like a personalization engine that offers a service to other components but might not be directly visible in the functional description.

The infrastructure view helps to identify software products that can be used for the different components. It helps to identify all products needed before modelling the requirements in the functional components.

HOW SOON WILL MY HOME BE A SMART HOME?

The barriers to mass market acceptance of the Smart Home are still high, but they are not insurmountable. Your home won't be a fully functional Smart Home by the end of this year, or even the end of next year.

But you will probably start to see more and more Smart elements in many more everyday homes. And perhaps when you get a critical mass of smart elements in your home, you will suddenly discover that you have a Smart Home without intending to do so.

The situation we have now with the Smart Home is that we know what we are missing. Market players are prepared and products are designed and prototyped. There is an ongoing discussion about the language that would permit "my object can talk with your object." And there is still a very early understanding of business roles and ecosystems in this context.

Yes, we are already there from a technology point of view.

The key issue is mindset—in the mindset of the telecoms, the mindset of the CE companies, the mindset of the service providers, and the mindset of the consumers as well.

It is all about a paradigm shift that recognizes different values in the future with a tremendous impact on any of the components; that is, the way to price a product, the way to provide a product to the customer, and the ecosystem needed to operate it in the required manner.

Let us take another example of a washing machine: Company X is well known as the best-of-breed washing machine manufacturer—long-life products, reliable, easy to maintain, low energy, good quality of washing. But the consumer's purchase decision is still recognition of value by the consumer with focus on these capabilities. This will be changing dramatically in a Smart Home environment. Washing may be just a commodity that can be provided by any washing machine; long life time is not anymore of value while enjoying the innovation cycles in technologies. The buying in the future might be based on the following:

- **Convenience.** While sitting in front of the TV, I always can see the status of washing.
- **Safety and security.** By using this washing machine, I get a better rate from my homeowner insurance.
- **Avoiding preinvestment.** Having bought service for 200 cycles and not the device itself, someone else is taking care of providing the detergent—as well as offering a replacement after four years.

It is all going to be about new business, new revenue streams, new behavior, and new solutions and products. One result of this could be a golden opportunity for early movers in the CE space to maintain customer loyalty based on this new kind of personal relationships with their consumers based on quality of services.

This new way of living in a Smart Home will require a number of new elements to fall into place. It will be paradigm shift experienced by CE companies, telecoms, and consumers, as well as the whole ecosystem. And it's going to take a while for all the parts to come together.

The day when everybody lives in a fully functional Smart Home is still well over the horizon.

CONCLUSION

The Smart Home seems to be appealing to many—at least everybody is asking for it. But before it becomes so irresistible that we see a widespread adoption, many things will have to happen. As often is the case, it is not about the technology, but about business models, service providers, ecosystems, and the right mindset. Back in the quiet seas of regulated markets, the Smart Home might have already materialized, but in the stormy waters of today's market, there are costs on several levels that make bringing the Smart Home into the port more of a challenge.

5

Telehealthcare: The Key to the Living Room

Hagen Wenzek, Derk Frank

At the intersection of medical devices, consumer electronics, Smart Home, and mobile communications, a relatively new segment has emerged: telehealthcare. This is "the use of telecommunications and information technologies to provide health care services at a distance, to include diagnosis, treatment, public health, consumer health information, and health professions education."[1] The following scenario highlights its importance.

"Oh, Grandmother, your personal health system sent me a text message that your weight changed more than 2 kilos (4.5 pounds) since yesterday. Did you eat too much?"

"My virtual assistant on the TV asked me the same, too. Seems to be the heart again, my child."

---

1. "Innovation, Demand, and Investment in Telehealth," *US Department of Commerce*, February, 2004.

"But, Grandmother, what can we do about it? I don't want to rush you to the emergency room again."

"My doctor called me as soon as I clicked the "Shortness of Breath" symptom button. She reminded me of the medicine she gave me when that happens."

"Is that enough, Grandmother?"

"I also need to get back to my rigid low-fat, low-salt diet and have my medication adjusted. Let us pick a recipe from my TV-assistant's suggestions and go shopping by foot."

"Oh, Grandmother, we have to watch your health status more closely."

"My doctor put me on the alert watch, and now a nurse looks even more often after my measurements and will come without asking as soon as anything changes for the worse. But she said I will be fine and should keep measuring blood pressure and heartbeat with my mobile phone even when we are shopping."

And scarcely had the grandma said this, than with one bound she was out of bed, and they bought fresh carrots, ginger, and parsley for their tasty and light Gingered Carrots.

Later the grandchild went joyously home, and Grandmother lived happily for many more years.[2]

This is no fairytale. It can save lives and a lot of money because electronics companies continuously explore new areas where they can apply innovative technology. However, markets that promised a large demand such as the Smart Home did not pick up as expected and remain sluggish. So players search for even more appealing applications that create enough interest to break the dead-lock. A swift scan of global opportunities creates a bright spot on the radar screen: medical applications. With the convergence of consumer electronics and medical devices, the field of telehealthcare provides

---

2.   Inspired by "Little Red Riding Hood," Grimm Brothers and the English translation by Margaret Hunt (www.fln.vcu.edu/grimm/redridinghood.html). Includes facts on Congestive Heart Failure from the American Heart Association (www.americanheart.org/presenter.jhtml?identifier=1486).

a promising and meaningful growth market. Not only that medical cost can be reduced dramatically, but successful solutions can even safe lives. With such a value proposition in hand, the additional push for the Smart Home comes without extra effort and can provide the missing key to the living room for CE companies.

REVENUE AND PROFIT IN CONSUMER ELECTRONICS

Rapid swings and huge dips in revenue growth for most CE areas over the next years are expected to be ruled by constantly slow growth. While peripherals such as printers, hard disks, keyboards, electrical components, and home entertainment products will enjoy revenue growth of at least five to six percent, for the white goods, personal communications and photo equipment segments, not more than one to two percent growth is expected[3] (see Figure 5.1). Therefore, companies are out there looking for other areas where electronics can play a significant role and attract new customers.

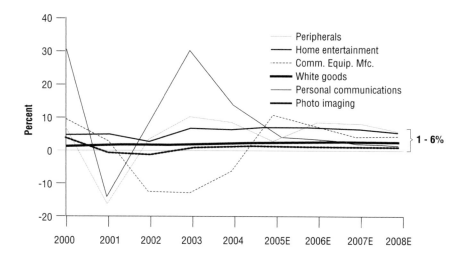

Figure 5.1   Consumer electronics related growth rates.

---

3.   IBM Market Intelligence analysis of company and analysts data.

One field that is closely monitored by many industry players, analysts, and the press is the living room. The tale of the Smart Home has been told many times, and companies did bet large sums on the rapid market expansion. However, so far that did not materialize. Still today, when analyzing the market, analysts focus on a few well-known application areas[4]—personal entertainment, consumer-driven devices, and the core services necessary to establish the infrastructure. Thus, the leading combatants monitored in this battlefield come from the cable, games, and PC industries. To actually make the digital home commercially real, applications need to move from "nice to have" to "meaningful." A compelling underlying business case becomes mandatory.

One such area that provides "meaningful" applications is clearly the medical segment. For a long time, companies offering products and solutions for healthcare enjoyed margins far beyond any other electronics product area. As recently as 2003, the average EBIT margin for medical device manufacturers was an astonishing 24% (see Figure 5.2). Compared with the next best segment of white goods where an EBIT margin of 6% could be realized, this seemed like a business on a different planet. This situation did not go unnoticed. Competition increased, and now the medical device segment has a still healthy but drastically reduced profit with only 12% EBIT margin in 2004. Due to further productivity gains and higher sales, telecommunications equipment manufacturers (16% EBIT) and semiconductor producers (13%) put medical on the third place of the profitability ranking of the electronics industry.[5]

Having that in mind, we see various solution providers and manufacturers moving into the ecosystem that has the closest relationship between consumer electronics and medical devices: telehealthcare.

---

4.   Schadler, Ted, "The Battle For The Digital Home," Forrester, 2004.
5.   IBM Institute for Business Value analysis of Factiva data.

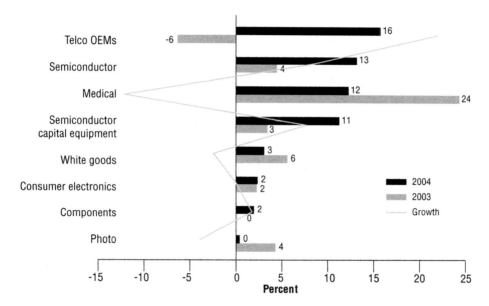

Figure 5.2 Average EBIT margins in electronics in 2003 and 2004.

ADVANCED MEDICAL TREATMENT

In our research, we are focusing on the remote monitoring of chronically ill patients in their homes or mobile environment via information technology. This includes the application of devices such as mobile phones, personal digital assistants, and intelligent medicine cabinets, as well as wirelessly connected scales, heartbeat monitors, and so forth to measure quantitative data.

With a continuous and automated monitoring of important vital parameters such as weight, blood pressure, heart frequency, or glucose levels, as well as surveys to capture qualitative data of the perceived condition of a patient, the treatment of various diseases becomes much more effective. Normally, only when they visit a doctor, patients get their health parameters measured. While this might lead to an instant intervention when the results indicate a decreasing health level, most of the time a slight downgrade goes unnoticed.

Then a sudden decompensation can invoke an emergency room visit. Hospital treatment will help the patient get back to a good health status. But as this is a chronic disease, the next emergency visit with more fatal consequences can already be anticipated.

Obviously, this treatment is both costly for the healthcare systems—few things are more expensive than an emergency room visit—as well as for the patient's quality of life. By continuously checking the vital parameters that can indicate a change of the health status (for CHF, a degrade is indicated, for example, by an increase of weight and blood pressure), a care manager can intervene proactively by advising on medication, nutrition, or through other appropriate means.[6]

Other diseases with similar potential for better treatment are asthma and diabetes. Most telehealthcare solutions on the market cover them, and we therefore focus on these three diseases in our further discussion of the topic.

ECOSYSTEM CONGESTION

With a telehealthcare solution, the crucial vital parameters can be measured, analyzed, presented to the care manager, and fed back to the patient. Such a solution consists of various devices that are connected to a hub that distributes the data electronically (Figure 5.3). Analytical tools and visualization applications not only make the data available to the various stakeholders but might also link it to other medical records of the patient. Appropriate user interfaces for the patient, the care manager, and even payer organizations or other interested and approved parties, obviously depending on the need, application and always in consistence with any relevant security, safety, and privacy aspects, enable a real interaction.

The technical part of telehealthcare attracts various manufacturers of sensors, communication devices, infrastructure, and pharmaceutical devices, but also PCs and home appliances. Analyzing the intentions of those parties to diversify into telehealthcare generates valuable insight about their strategies and potential.

---

6. Jessup, Mariell, Brozena, Susan, "Heart Failure," *The New England Journal of Medicine*, May 15, 2003, pp. 2007-2018.

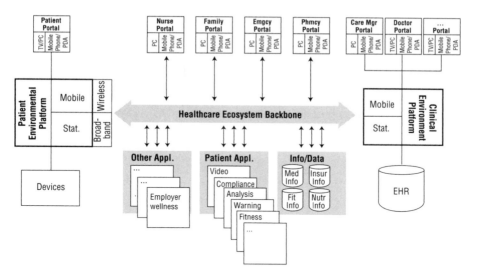

Figure 5.3   Ecosystem view of the telehealthcare value net.

It has already been discussed that consumer electronic companies need to go into new markets with new products to achieve more than just marginal revenue growth. For pharmaceutical companies, however, the situation is different. Their current product portfolio (drugs and some measuring devices) has more substantial limitations: New blockbuster drugs are not in sight, patents for many profitable drugs expire, and the effectiveness of drugs under current treatment plans is questionable.[7] As the Vice President of GlaxoSmithKline, Alan Roses points out, "The vast majority of drugs—more than 90 percent—only work in 30 or 50 percent of the people."[8] With a direct feedback loop from the patient through remote monitoring, a much more targeted treatment is possible. Something that is known as "targeted treatment solutions" describe "products and therapeutic healthcare packages that include diagnostic tests, drugs, and monitoring devices and mechanisms, as well as a wide range of services to support patients."[9]

7.   "Pharma 2010: The threshold of innovation," *IBM Institute for Business Value*, Somers, NY, 2004.

8.   Connor, Steve, "Glaxo Chief: Our Drugs Do Not Work on Most Patients," *The Independent,* UK, 2003-12-08.

9.   "Pharma 2010: The threshold of innovation," *IBM Institute for Business Value,* Somers, NY, 2004.

With these few examples, it already becomes clear that the ecosystem telehealthcare resides in is highly competitive, underlies strong dynamics, sees many different partnerships or alliances, and is an opportunity in an already quite congested space. Electronic companies that want to be successful in such an area need to thoroughly understand what their value proposition would be, how their business case has to be developed, and what role they can play.

TECHNOLOGICAL MATURITY

By combining the low cost, ease of use, and widespread penetration of consumer electronics devices with the clinical robustness and medical viability of healthcare devices, a new family of solutions is ready for widespread application. Medical devices like glucose meters or ECG monitors have achieved a level of miniaturization and integration where they can be economically brought to the patient's home. Some of these medical devices have already become consumer electronics commodities, such as simple but effective heart rate monitors and blood pressure devices. And even entertainment products have become powerful enough to be used for mobile medical applications.

X-RAYS ON AN IPOD

Just have a look what the Apple iPod, one of the most successful CE devices of the last few years, is able to offer: OsiriX, an open platform for handling medical images, has been adapted to work on the iPod.[10] There the doctor can view and freely rotate those same 3D images that reside on the stationary workstation. This makes the iPod a cheap and handy device to discuss clinical results with the patient or colleague. The user interface is intuitive, and the solution is unconstrained by networks or fixed work places.

---

10. homepage.mac.com/rossetantoine/osirix/Index2.html.

Solutions such as Motiva from Philips,[11] Biotronik Home Monitoring,[12] or IBM's mHealth[13] toolkit show that technology is mature enough to constantly collect relevant vital data. Off the shelf medical devices are linked wirelessly to a mobile or stationary hub from where data is transferred to a server. Besides dedicated software for the analysis or the connection into a clinical environment, all components are widely available and of a price comparable to standard consumer electronics.

USABILITY

A typical objection against such a high-tech treatment is that patients are required to actively deal with technology. People question the ability of elderly to do so. However, one should not underestimate the spreading experience. We have examined the different patient groups, as follows.[14]

Twenty-five percent of the maximum number of hospitalizations for the four diseases under investigation (see Figure 5.4) happen at an age of 45–50. Here we can assume that technology is a normal part of life if these patients do not belong to other special groups, too, such as blind, deaf, with Alzheimer's disease, and so forth. Any solution that resembles the technological sophistication of a simple TV remote control or normal telephone will have a high probability to gain acceptance.

11. www.medical.philips.com/main/products/telemonitoring/products/motiva.
12. www.biotronik.com.
13. Husemann, Dirk, Narayanaswami, Chandra, Nidd, Mike, "Personal Mobile Hub" in: *Proc of 8th Intl Symposium on Wearable Computers (ISWC)*, 2004, pp. 85-91.
14. IBM Institute for Business Value analysis of German statistical data (Statistisches Bundesamt).

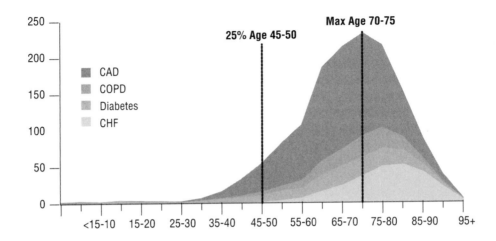

Figure 5.4 Hospitalization by disease, Germany, 2004.

However, the majority of hospital admissions happen during the age of 70–75 (data for Germany). These patients currently have rather low technological experience. But if we look closer at the group in between (50–64 years), it will drastically improve in the next five to 10 years. The Kaiser family foundation found for the US that some 70 percent of people in this group already have some Internet experience.[15] As these people get older and more become patients, we can assume their much higher comfort level with technology.

Nevertheless, making the solution as simple to install and use as possible will continue to be a critical prerequisite for acceptance. Even if people are technology savvy in their normal life, the disease might simply prevent them from handling a more complicated system.

---

15. "e-Health and the Elderly: How Seniors Use the Internet for Health—Survey," *Kaiser Family Foundation,* www.kff.org/entmedia/entmedia011205pkg.cfm.

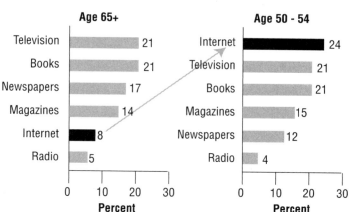

Figure 5.5 Media usage to gather medical information.

CLINICAL EFFECTIVENESS

While it sounds reasonable that a continuous measurement of vital data and a proactive intervention by a care manager upon a degrading health status prevents hospital visits, can it also be scientifically proven? The current literature provides a mixed picture: While various clinical studies indicate a reduction in hospitalization due to telehealthcare of at least 28 percent[16] for Coronary Artery Disease (CAD) and up to 75 percent[17] for cases with Diabetes, in meta-studies technical flaws in the underlying studies have been pointed out.[18] For instance, the number of

16. "Independent Analysis of Monitored/Non-Monitored Patients, January 1, 2002 through March 31, 2004," *SHP—Strategic Healthcare Programs*, Santa Barbara, CA, 2004.

17. Ibid.

18. Gonseth, Jonas. et al., "The effectiveness of disease management programs in reducing hospital re-admission in older patients with heart failure: a systematic review and meta-analysis of published reports," Eur Heart J. 2004; 25: 1570-1595 and May, Carl. et al., "Telemedicine and the 'Future Patient'? Risk, Governance and Innovation," www.york.ac.uk/res/iht/projects/1218252067/MayFinalRptSummaryRefs.pdf.

patients is too low, or the duration of the study too short. These negative statements lead to a restriction of reimbursement by payer organizations for a telehealthcare-based treatment of those diseases.

However, the growing number of trials, increasing penetration of telehealthcare solutions, and the results of existing studies lead to a high probability that a large, randomized, and broadly recognized study will indeed validate the existing results. Therefore, an electronics company that does not want to miss the market opportunity needs to understand in depth what the business case would probably look like—and then act upon the results. With so many interested parties congesting the marketplace, waiting for those solid and proven results might prohibit any business success at all. Upon availability, payer organizations, medical providers, and patients will then act swiftly. Those electronics companies that can deliver a mature product will be able to grab the lion share of the market.

SAVINGS OF MEDICAL EXPENDITURES

With prevalence between 3 and 13 percent in the age group over 65 years, CHF alone leads to over 260,000 hospitalizations in Germany or about 1 million in the US.[19] With an average cost of $13,500 for those typical 14 days in hospital, the direct burden for the healthcare systems is $3.5 billion per year. In the US, a cost of $11 billion is estimated.[20] The question is then raised . . . how much could telehealthcare save?

GROSS SAVINGS

Existing studies analyze the effectiveness of telehealthcare for three diseases that on the one hand contribute significantly to the

19. Gheorghiade, Mihai, Bonow, Robert O., "Chronic Heart Failure in the United States," *Circulation*. 1998; 97:p. 282-289.
20. Ibid.

overall healthcare costs and on the other hand can be monitored by a very small variety of devices. In a simple setting, CHF, Asthma, and Diabetes require not more than a scale, heart beat monitor, blood pressure cuff, an ECG, and a glucose meter.

By focusing on two parameters for the reduction of inpatient care, namely hospitalization and emergency care visits, the baseline for the gross savings estimation can be laid out. The upswing potential comes through outpatient treatment reductions such as ambulant visits, nursing beds, and so forth. We have exemplarily analyzed hospitalization for CHF in Germany, as follows.

CASE STUDY—GERMAN HEALTHCARE COSTS SAVINGS

Studies that measure the impact of telehealthcare indicate a reduction of at least "3–4 days"[21] in the hospital per year, up to "50 percent reduction,"[22] with more studies leaning to the higher numbers. A conservative estimation of reduction in hospitalization of 38 percent results in a gross saving potential of over $5,000 per year per patient. This would mean over $600 million for the healthcare system of Germany alone.[23] Adding the figures of a German insurer, that is a payer organization, Taunus BKK has used for their roll-out[24]—70 percent less emergency care visits and respectively lower hospitalization rates—the gross savings for Germany's healthcare system could nearly be $2 billion or €1.5 billion.

21. Cox, Robert, "Monitoring Chronic Disease in the Home: Clinical and Financial Observations," www.atmeda.org/news/2004_presentations/m1d3.cox.ppt.
22. Ryan, Patricia, "Patient Centered Outcomes of Diabetes Care: Technology and Care Coordination", www.atmeda.org/news/2004_presentations/m1d4.Ryan.ppt.
23. Assuming a rate of hospitalization rate per patient per year of 2.2.
24. "Neuer Vertrag deckt Telemedizin für chronisch Herzkranke ab," Ärztezeitung 2005-03-25.

NET SAVINGS

Against these gross savings stand costs for the telehealthcare solution. Currently available commercial offers as well as business case calculations by IBM indicate a price of $130–200 per patient per month.[25] When all patients leaving a hospital would receive a telehealthcare solution, a maximum of $600,000 would have to be spent (in our case for Germany),[26] assuring an almost instant return on investment (ROI). And even if all patients with CHF would receive a telehealthcare solution regardless of a hospital visit, the ROI would be flat, "only" saving lives.[27] But even here a rapid increase in net savings happens when taking further parameters (for instance fewer emergency room admissions, less emergency car sorties, reduction of post discharge visits, reduction of outpatient visits) and diseases into account. As, for example, CHF and Diabetes often occur simultaneously, just adding a glucose meter to a "CHF-kit" enables monitoring and treatment of that disease, too.

RECOMMENDATIONS

Telehealthcare has the potential to become one of the primary pillars of the global medical systems extending the traditional in- and outpatient treatment, as shown in Figure 5.6.

Costs are lower as fewer hospital stays are needed, less emergency situations occur, and nurses have to visit the patient less often.

---

25. "Neuer Vertrag deckt Telemedizin für chronisch Herzkranke ab," *Ärztezeitung* 2005-03-25.
26. This assumes a rehospitalization rate per year of 1; i.e. each hospitalization per year is attributed to a different patient, even though many patients visit the hospital more than once per year, thus decreasing the total number of different patients and therefore required telehealthcare kits. However, we continue to calculate with the most conservative number and the highest price for the solution of $200 per patient per month.
27. One study found the mortality to be reduced by 43% [European Union project TEN-HMS].

Treatment is better as it is based on more reliant, long-term patient data, and patients' compliance and persistence with medication is increased.

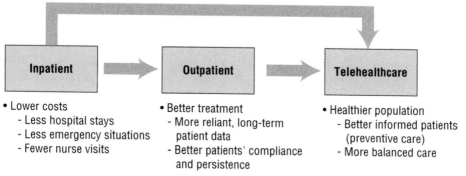

• Lower costs
  - Less hospital stays
  - Less emergency situations
  - Fewer nurse visits

• Better treatment
  - More reliant, long-term patient data
  - Better patients' compliance and persistence

• Healthier population
  - Better informed patients (preventive care)
  - More balanced care

• Other
- Free up doctor's time from administrative to more value added work
- Helping improve the profile of the healthcare system

Figure 5.6   Long-term advantages of a fully embedded telehealthcare treatment.

A population becomes healthier as people are better informed about their state of health, achieving more balanced care.

STUDY

However, medical, payer, and patient communities will only broadly recognize these benefits when fully accepted and scientifically sound studies are published. Studies conducted up to now typically lack one or more of the following critical success factors:

- Placebo-controlled (if ethically tenable and technically feasible) double-blind trial.

- Large scale (to reach significant results even with little differences).

- Hard endpoints: for example, death.

- Published in internationally known, widely read, and highly cited journals (high "impact factor").

Telehealthcare still relies on strong and persistent persuasion and business development (a typical market push-model). This led to multiple island implementations, pilots, or prototypes. For an electronics company, conducting such a study will most probably be out of scope. Partnering among institutions from academia and medical providers and payers has the potential to establish the credibility of telehealthcare to create a market pull where stakeholders find their own value proposition such as the following:

- Medical doctors want to provide more successful treatment.

- Payer organizations want to spend less.

- Patients want to be healthier.

CLINICAL ENVIRONMENT OR INTERACTION CENTERS

Electronics companies are best positioned to provide equipment, infrastructure, and non-medical services for a telehealthcare solution. While the patient's environment is rather straightforward to handle, many solutions fail when it comes to integrating them into the clinical environment. In an advanced hospital or clinic that has widespread usage of IT, the doctor will deal with the PC in his daily routine already many times. Alerts and an aggregated visual representation of remotely monitored patient data can be seamlessly embedded into the normal workflow.

However, many hospitals lack such a modern infrastructure and are still heavily paper-based. Adding a PC or an additional workplace to the doctor's routine will cause extra time and thus usually will cause objections. Here, only when a separate center takes over the whole analysis, first and second level care, this becomes a feasible approach. The medical doctor at the treating hospital will only be consulted when the results are unclear or a change in medication becomes necessary. Additional long-term data will be provided, for example monthly, to enable a more targeted treatment of the patient.

Further on, existing infrastructure available to the doctor and other care personnel has to be taken into account. For advanced disease management, IT savvy care takers use PDAs to manage their schedules, access digital health records, and so forth. Any application therefore needs to seamlessly integrate with these existing devices—something that is possible, for example, with state-of-the-art Webservices models. Handing out another device however, is out of the question.

HOME ENVIRONMENT

The infrastructure, from the broadband connections to the residential gateways and hubs is discussed in detail in Chapter 4, "The Smart Home: Coming to Your House Soon, but Not Too Soon." Companies that want to develop cost-effective telehealthcare solutions will base their architecture on this concept—either to leverage existing infrastructure, to use economies of scale for the components, or to enable the integration of further value added services when the infrastructure is in place.

However, consider some special conditions.

The *exchange of medical data* has to adhere to certain standards. Unfortunately, these are neither globally consistent nor mature. Areas to consider are, for instance:

- **Privacy.** The US Health Insurance Portability and Accountability Act (HIPAA) sets standards for e-Health including privacy and security concerns.

- **Interoperability.** HL7 provides standards for the transmission of patient information between disparate electronic health records (EHR).

- **Communications.** IEEE 11073 / ISO TC251 defines how point of care devices are managed.

Legal aspects might also restrict the processing of data. For example, some countries prohibit the export of patient data to other countries—something that would automatically happen in centralized installations or through the outsourcing of data processing to offshore countries, if not addressed explicitly.

SELECT BUSINESS PARTNERS CAREFULLY

Disease Management data from German patients that is captured in forms was sent by a document service provider for further processing to Vietnam. There, the data was manually transformed into a different format and sent back to Germany. However, contracts and law prohibit such a transmission of patient data outside the country. The case became public in the media and was discussed in the German parliament.[28]

The *user interface* needs to be tailored for elderly people with various diseases. While we have seen that a Web front-end becomes more and more of an option, using a mobile phone for anything other than data capture and transfer is unpractical. Keys and the display are already cumbersome to use for many young, healthy persons. Using the well-accepted TV set as a primary user interface is, on the other side, a very straightforward device. The mobile phone could then be used while outside of the home with few controls for very limited interaction.

Installation and maintenance has to be focused on self-service to the widest extent. Any visit by technical personnel not only quickly degrades the business case, but also jeopardizes the customer satisfaction.

MARKET AND PLATFORM STRATEGY

We have analyzed 20 solutions that are available on the market today or have only recently been announced and found just two to be based on an open platform concept. The rest use proprietary interfaces, devices, applications, and/or services. The providers of

---

28. Deutscher Bundestag, 2005-04-13, www.petra-pau.de/15_bundestag/ dok/down/15168_05_04_13_Pau_mfr_disease-management.pdf; "Monitor," WDR, 2005-03-17, www.wdr.de/tv/monitor/ beitrag.phtml?bid=669&sid=126.

those solutions follow a classical dominator strategy: They try to lock the client into a specific solution preventing the usage of any other technology, application, or service.

While this might lead to the highest profits in the short term, it imposes risks and has disadvantages for the whole ecosystem, thus effectively reducing the long-term opportunity for the provider, as well:

■ The receiving side of the ecosystem (payers, medical providers, patients) does not resonate well to a dominating company and is highly fragmented.

■ Telehealthcare is only one component of an IT-enabled healthcare system where no company can control all the assets by themselves.

■ Innovation in technology, services, or the business model itself cannot to come from the provider alone.

As laid out in the IBM IBV whitepaper, "Rewiring Electronics," as well as in other publications,[29] a platform concept based on a so-called *keystone strategy* has significantly more potential for long-term success. Here, the telehealthcare solution would consist of one or more open platforms to provide basic infrastructure services (owned by the keystone company) and advanced services built upon this or these platforms by niche players. As the platform and its interfaces are open and preferably standardized, the integration of core value added services, such as blood pressure reading, trend analysis, and compliance reminders can be achieved seamlessly. But also non-core services such as Internet access, video telephony, or multimedia feedback can become part of the overall value proposition without extra effort.

---

29. Iansiti, Marco, Levien, Roy, "The Keystone Advantage: What the New Dynamics of Business Ecosystems Mean for Strategy, Innovation, and Sustainability." *Harvard Business School Press,* Boston, MA, 2004, and Göthlich, Stephan "From Loosely Coupled Systems to Collaborative Business Ecosystems." Paper No. 573, University of Kiel. May 2003. www.bwl.uni-kiel.de/bwlinstitute/grad-kolleg/de/kollegiaten/goethlich/Business%20Ecosystems%204b%201,5Z.pdf

KEYSTONE CONCEPT (EXCERPT FROM "REWIRING ELECTRONICS")

A keystone understands the role of other keystones and the contributions of niche players, evaluating the ability of partner organizations to innovate and utilize resources and services as a distributed effort. Acting as an ecosystem hub, the keystone connects partner organizations via common standards and makes the flow of information transparent. The keystone's focus is not on controlling the marketplace but on attracting other organizations by creating platforms and sharing solutions. The keystone strives to sustain value creation while balancing value extraction and sharing.

Instead of trying to dominate the entire competitive landscape, keystones strive to establish innovation strategies that facilitate the overall health of the ecosystem. To differentiate against dominators, keystones promote openness and collaboration among organizations within the ecosystem by establishing platforms and services that innovators can tap into.

The role of the keystone will therefore often be the general contractor to hospitals or payer organizations, the orchestrator of the value proposition, and the maintainer of the platform as well as its interfaces.

Overall, the telehealthcare ecosystem has all the attributes that make it receptive for a keystone strategy:

- Networks are formed by more and more loosely coupled companies rather than tightly coupled pairs of buyers and suppliers.
- Assets that are directly or indirectly part of the solution are not all owned by the one contract partner and therefore impossible to fully control.
- Healthcare applications require a breadth of services and innovation that no company can effectively and efficiently provide on their own.

Therefore, one has the full potential to leverage the benefits attributed to a keystone approach:

- Superior innovation as niche players with new and better services are constantly attracted.

- Closer fit with the requirements from all stakeholders as a reconfiguration of the solution can be done cost effectively.

- Greater probability that the whole ecosystem will grow—and the participants will be able to grow with it.

CONCLUSION

Healthcare systems are at a collapse. If we don't broadly embrace technology, which is already state of the art in basically all other industries, costs become unbearable for our economies. At the same time, electronics companies are on the hunt for new ways to apply their capabilities. It could be a perfect fit—but the CE companies have to acknowledge the special character of the healthcare system. If they can establish the right networks to create the pull of the stakeholders, telehealthcare will become a major factor in treating and preventing the most costly diseases. And what better value proposition to make your home smarter can you have than a doctor's prescription?

Online Gaming Environments: People, Technology, Money, and Social Networks

Andreas Neus, Mike West

Using computers to play games is now commonplace. Mr. Smith plays simulated golf on his computer, Mrs. Smith plays blackjack, their teenage son, Robbie, plays role games with others over the Internet, and their daughter, Sarah, is limited to educational games because she is still in elementary school. The Smiths have two computers and a game console. Most of the time, they use those machines to play games.

Gaming like this is a phenomenon that didn't exist 30 years ago, except in a handful of universities. But games have been a key part of the personal computer revolution and of consumer electronics in general.

As computers and dedicated gaming machines become even more powerful, we will have the ingredients for a dramatic transformation within the entertainment industry. We can expect the more traditional entertainment of video, film, and audio to combine with games to give us a completely different entertainment experience.

When we talk about gaming, we mean the following:

■ Dedicated video game consoles (the dominant games platform in the US).

■ Personal computers (the dominant platform for gaming in Europe and Asia).

■ Game-capable mobile platforms.

The games themselves also come in several shapes and sizes, as listed in Table 6.1.

Table 6.1 Game Types

Game Type	Connection Type	Example Games
Single Player	None	Knights of the Old Republic
Local Two-Player	Split Screen, Direct Connection, WLAN Gran Tourismo 3	
Multiplayer (<32)	Peer-to-Peer via LAN or Internet	CounterStrike, Half-Life 2
Massively Multiplayer	Client-Server via Internet	World of Warcraft, Star Wars Galaxies

Games scale from traditional single-player games to two-player games (shared-screen or direct connection) and multiplayer games—played via (W)LAN or Internet—up to massively multiplayer online games (MMOG), which are hosted on dedicated server infrastructure, providing a persistent game world simultaneously to tens of thousands of players over the Internet.

The expanding capabilities and increasing number of games-specific and games-capable platforms, coupled with the worldwide proliferation of low-latency Internet access, have enabled the recent boost of multiplayer and massively multiplayer games. These trends will likely yield new forms of entertainment, new virtual communities, and new environments of communication and commerce.

TECHNOLOGY AND THE "GAMES COMPUTER"

Unlike the constant stream of incremental advances that characterize the PC market, the video games console market is cyclical, with new generations of game systems being brought to market every four to five years.

A given games console design has a product life of up to seven years, during which time the performance of that games console remains constant.

By the late 1990s, when studying technology trends in the games market, we found that the performance of video games consoles was rising dramatically from one generation to the next. Examining the performance of games consoles over several generations, performance (across several different metrics) and performance requirements continue to rise faster than that of general purpose computers (such as PCs) and at a rate that is faster than "Moore's Law" (see the sidebar in Chapter 2, "The New Role of Technology and Services in Next Generation Businesses").

By the onset of the 2005–2006-generation of video games consoles, it became clear that the performance of games console processors would actually far exceed the most powerful and expensive processors found in PCs (see Figure 6.1). The challenging question was how to achieve this performance while still maintaining a price point commensurate with a consumer electronics (CE) product.

Requirements of games applications differ significantly from those of general purpose computing. Parallelism and pipelines are in the nature of games processing. This "Games Problem" allows various processing tasks to be divided across multiple smaller processors rather than being confined less efficiently onto a single complex central processor. Multiple smaller processors amplify computer power. Such a chip is very powerful, but still affordable (see Chapter 8, "IBM's Global Technology Outlook and Its Implication to Consumer Electronics").

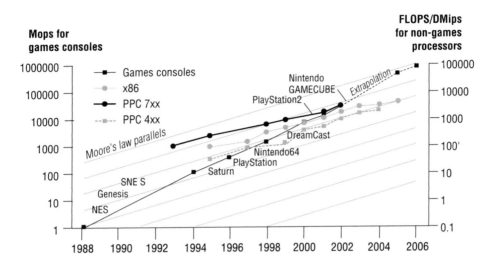

Figure 6.1 Game processors are catching up to general purpose microprocessors.

Similar technology trends are also occurring with the other chips of a games platform—namely the graphics and system functions. The recent advance in 3D graphics capability, both on the PC and in games consoles, has been dramatic, with high-end graphics chips reaching the same level of complexity as processor chips. High-performance designs increasingly consist of multiple (four, eight, or even more) simultaneously operating "graphics pipelines" that perform 3D geometry, lighting, and texture mapping computations that render synthetic visual images of stunning quality and realism.

Fuelled by the rapid advancement of technology, the capabilities of all gaming platforms, PCs, consoles, and a wide variety of mobile platforms, will continue to increase dramatically.

TO PLAY A BETTER GAME?

With the stunning visual realism of the new games and all that computing power behind it, will the gaming experience automatically improve?

All the technology in the world is no guarantee of more entertainment or better games. In the same way, more special effects are no guarantee of a better movie, and a better page layout and cover design is no guarantee of a better novel. Even if physically accurate and beautifully rendered, a poor game remains a poor game despite the greatest technology available. A great game will always be a great game, largely independent of the technical merits of the platform, but the developer can make a great game even better by exploiting the attributes of a great platform.

Technology is to a game developer what brushes and a palette are to an artist. Both uniquely use their media to communicate with an audience and capture their imagination. Across every aspect of the game, the developer seeks to provide the little touches that extend the suspension of disbelief.

But to be successful, the game must be "fun," providing the right level of stimulation and entertainment plus a strong sense of achievement on completion of objectives.

WHAT ELSE CAN WE DO?

Connectivity is coming to a games platform near you. In fact, it's probably already there.

With the rise of the Internet over the last 15 years and the increasing affordability of home networking, there is little surprise that the PC continues to lead the way in games connectivity. Until recently, online gaming has been solely a PC-based phenomenon.

But games consoles already incorporate connectivity, either fully integrated or as an add-on accessory feature. And the manufacturers apply more and more emphasis to connectivity, both for Internet and local networks, with every new generation.

MARKET OVERVIEW & TRENDS

The comparison of the US $10 billion video game industry overtaking Hollywood box-office revenues in 2003 was impressive and has often been cited.[1] But that figure is somewhat skewed due to inclusion of hardware on the game side and the exclusion of DVD and other revenue streams on the movie side. However, it is still an interesting milestone showing that computer games are not a fringe phenomenon.

ACCELERATED SALES

The massively multiplayer game *World of Warcraft*—which can only be played online with or against other players—became the fastest-selling PC game in North America in 2004/2005. It sold 240,000 copies through retailers within the first 24 hours. Three months later in Europe that was topped with 280,000 copies. More records were broken a month later, with 1.5 million subscribers worldwide and a peak of more than half a million concurrent users.

With $50 for the game CD, and a monthly subscription fee of about $14, Blizzard Corporation can capture over $300 million in the first year from this title alone.

Adoption rates for multiplayer games have also been rising rapidly over the last decade (see Figure 6.2). Comparing major MMOG releases since 1997, we find that the time required to reach 200,000 subscribers has dropped from 39 months to less than 1 month over the seven-year period.

Likewise, the peak number of subscribers has risen significantly over time, with *World of Warcraft* attracting more than seven times the previous *Everquest* peak by mid-2005 (see Figure 6.3).

---

1. Yi, Matthew, "THEY GOT GAME," *San Francisco Chronicle,* December. 18, 2004.

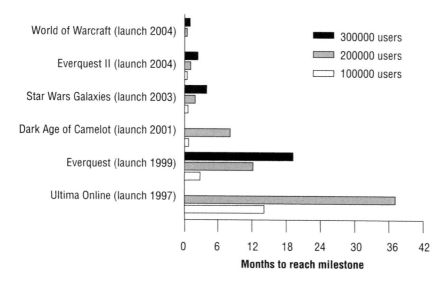

Figure 6.2 Adoption rate of massive multiplayer online games.[2]

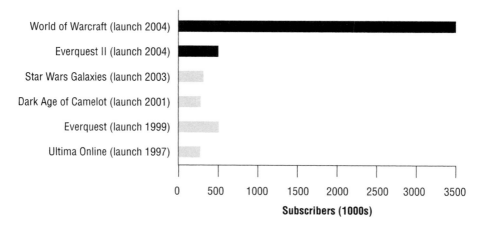

Figure 6.3 Peak subscriber numbers of major massively multiplayer online games.[3]

2. Based on Woodcock, Bruce Sterling S., "An Analysis of MMOG Subscription Growth," www.mmogchart.com. "EverQuest II Reaches 500,000 Users," Gametrailers.com, August 1, 2005. "WORLD OF WARCRAFT® REACHES 1.5 MILLION PAYING CUSTOMERS IN CHINA," Press Release Blizzard, July 20, 2005.

3. Ibid.

Given this data, it would seem that MMOGs may have reached a tipping point in 2004 and are moving from the fringe into a mainstream phenomenon. This is also supported by current primary research that the Media & Entertainment Strategy team of IBM Business Consulting Services has conducted in collaboration with the center for evaluation and methods (*Zentrum für Evaluation and Methoden*—ZEM) at Bonn University in a study representative for German consumers aged 14 to 39.

While less than 16 percent of the above 20-year-olds with Internet access were playing online games, this number skyrocketed to an astonishing 44 percent among the youngest age group of 14 to 19 year olds. Online gaming is no longer a niche (see Figure 6.4).

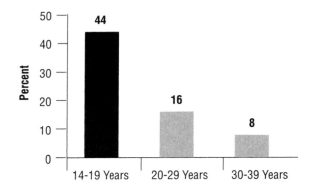

Figure 6.4   Usage of online games among young Internet users in Germany.[4]

MULTIPLAYER GAME DYNAMICS

The success and stickiness of multiplayer games rests on dynamics tying into players' communication and collaboration habits.

In the next several paragraphs, we will analyze some of these dynamics and show that they help people attribute social meaning and relevance to their virtual existence.

---

4.   IBM Medienstudie 2005, IBM Business Consulting Services & ZEM Bonn University.

COMMUNICATION

Collaboration requires communication. Most online games provide text-based chat interfaces to facilitate communication among fellow team members. As high-bandwidth and low-latency Internet connections become more economical and ubiquitous, natural voice (via voice-over IP) is increasingly used by gamers to communicate. Natural voice can provide a much richer and deeper experience, further blurring the borders between game and reality.

COOPERATION

Many MMOGs provide a way for players to self-organize into guilds, clans, or tribes. Given enough in-game currency, these may also be able to buy virtual real-estate in the form of guildhalls or castles. To encourage cooperation, many MMOG providers set up special quests that are only practical to tackle using a mixed team of different characters.

CROSSING THE GAME-WORLD BORDER

A sad example of an event where the border between the game environment and the real world was breached was the recent case of a Shanghai online game player who stabbed to death a competitor who sold the cyber-sword he had been lent for approximately US $800.[5] But there are also more joyous events, as in many MMOGs, people will follow rituals and traditions established in the virtual world, like rites of passage or even marriage ceremonies.

VIRTUAL VERSUS REAL WORLDS

We see mounting evidence that the use of traditional media among young consumers is being impacted by the success of online gaming. Especially teenagers between 14 and 19 years reduce their TV consumption and use the Internet more for online gaming and interactive chats than any other generation

---

5. "Online gamer killed for selling cyber sword," Reuters, March 30, 2005.

(see Figures 6.5 and 6.6). And multiplayer gaming is moving to become an organized spectator sport with prize-money for some tournaments already topping one million US dollars.

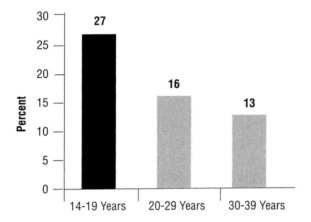

Figure 6.5   The share of German consumers who state their TV consumption has dropped due to the Internet is largest in the youngest age group.[6]

MAKING GAMING PAY

The idea of paying money to improve your chances in a multi-player game is not altogether new.

Wizards of the Coast used this paying mechanism to turn their hybrid trading card/card game, *Magic: The Gathering*, first released in 1993, into one of the best-selling games of all time. In their case, the powerful and somewhat addictive mechanism of paying for "items" (new, stronger cards) to tilt the game in one's favor was an integral part of the business model. In the case of MMOGs, it has proven to be an emergent market that many publishers are struggling to control.

---

6.   IBM Medienstudie 2005, IBM Business Consulting Services & ZEM Bonn University, IBM Stuttgart, Germany, 2005.

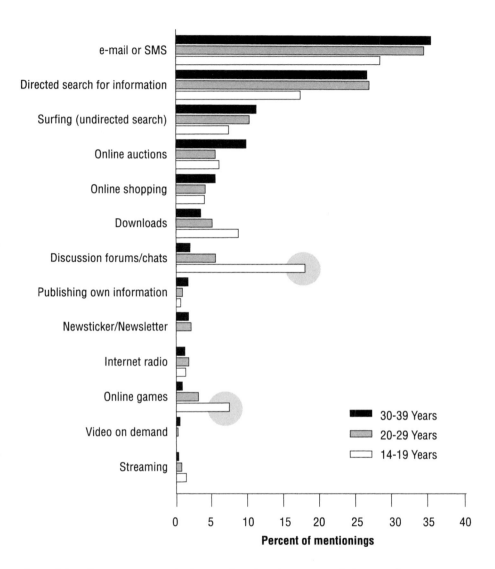

Figure 6.6   The two most popular Internet functions by age group in Germany.[7]

---

7.   Ibid.

Ultima Online, Everquest, and other massively multiplayer online games have spawned their own economy. Castranova calculated that already back in 2001, a player could "earn" US $3.43 per hour by playing *Everquest* and selling gained items on eBay.[8] Aggregated, sales of virtual artefacts and characters now go into the millions of US dollars. For example, eBay category 1645— "Internet Games," where many game-items are traded, showed sales of over $22 million in 2004, as Castronova has tallied (see Figure 6.7).

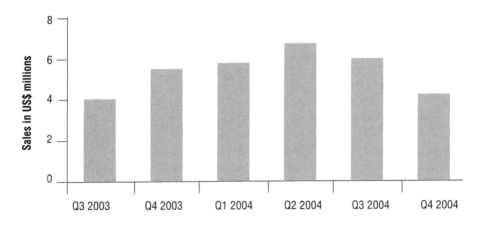

Figure 6.7   Sales in eBay category 1645, "Internet Games," at the end of 2004.[9]

This development has prompted the appearance of dedicated companies offering game artifacts and character-levelling services for money. This is not popular with game publishers, most of whom define in-game items and characters as their property, and some of whom are taking steps to curb this practice. For example, WoW

---

8.   Castronova, Edward, mypage.iu.edu/%7Ecastro/home.html.
9.   Ibid.

has recently deleted over 1,000 accounts that were used for professional "gold-farming" with the intent to sell the virtual gold to other players in exchange for real money.[10] Activities like professional gold-farming for money can upset the balance of the complex in-game economy, based on the in-game buying and selling of rare items (which were "earned" killing computer-controlled adversaries) in exchange for game currency. For instance, the complex in-game economy of *Ultima Online* had to be re-balanced a number of times by adjusting factors like the pay-out rates for items sold to non-player-characters, re-spawning of monsters, and the quality of the dropped items.[11]

But game balance being disturbed by a shadow-economy outside the game is only one of the issues. While game publishers may be looking at the commission revenue eBay generates trading game-items as money they could be making instead, there are a number of issues to resolve before a trade of items for real-world currency are likely to be officially supported by major games within the game platform. One concern is that officially supporting this kind of "sale" would require the game publishers to invest heavily in setting up and running an infrastructure and non-repudiation transaction system and disaster recovery procedures much like that of a major bank.

With in-game items often selling for four-figure sums on eBay, losing a character or items due to a bug or a server crash could expose the game service provider to significant damages claims. Likewise, all games we have seen so far exhibit a lifecycle—what would happen if the publisher decided to sunset a game? Overnight, all game items would lose their value.

Of course two industries exist in the real world where such losses are expected and accepted in the normal course of operations, and

---

10. "WORLD OF WARCRAFT® SETS NEW MILESTONE WITH 1.5 MILLION SUBSCRIBERS WORLDWIDE," Press Realease Blizzard, Irvine, CA, March 17, 2005. www.blizzard.com/press/031705-worldwide.shtml.

11. Vex, "Vex Comments: Real Economics in a Virtual World," *Origin*, November 10, 2003. update.uo.com/dev-comments.html.

that we believe could provide valuable insights and guidance to companies moving into trading of in-game items:

- One is the stock market, which can crash or where the value of an individual stock can be destroyed overnight, as it is a bet on the future value of a right. This model could work in the game context too.

- The other industry has created cities like Las Vegas and provides a steady revenue stream for many states . . . gambling. In gambling, people actually accept that losing money is part of the game.

But neither of these models releases game companies from having to become banks for all practical purposes: Casinos could not get away with simply taking all the money on a Roulette table and argue "technical difficulties," and neither could a stock exchange.

We see first steps to re-gain the revenue currently moving through eBay as commissions: Sony's Exchange Station provides an auction platform within the game provider's infrastructure and will charge a commission for each trade.[12] And in its *World of Warcraft MMOG*, Blizzard has effectively provided an in-game alternative for eBay— the Auction Houses. Here, players can put items up for auctions (for a commission paid to the Auction House in game-currency), and other players can bid for the items using game-currency.

ADVERTISING

In-game advertising is already a reality. *Electronic Arts* stated that it has made US $10 million in in-game-advertising revenues. And the recent *Splinter Cell: Chaos Theory* game contained ads by AMD, AXE, and Nokia.[13]

---

12. stationexchange.station.sony.com.
13. "Ubisoft Announces In-Game Advertising Partners for Tom Clancy's Splinter Cell Chaos Theory," *Gameinfowire*, April 4, 2005, gameinfowire.com/news.asp?nid=6095.

Reaction to product placement has been mostly favourable from the gaming community—under the provision that the advertising is incorporated in a non-intrusive fashion. Of course, players don't want to see a modern-day brand logo on a broadsword in a medieval fantasy setting, but in games set in a present or future context, provided it's handled with care, advertising can even increase the sense of realism. For instance, when walking past a soft drink vending machine in a tactical first-person-shooter, having a Coke or Pepsi logo on the machine may even result in a more realistic experience than a non-existing brand invented for use in the game. The non-existent and therefore unfamiliar brand can remind the player that this is not real, thereby impacting the depth of immersion in the game.

The same is true, of course, for sports games such as soccer or racing, where we have become so used to seeing the advertising that not having it would appear strange. As games become more convincing, immersive, and interactive, the possibilities for product placement in games become virtually limitless—and the possibility of interaction with the brand versus the traditional passive consumption of a TV commercial a real benefit. As an example, players might be taught (or even forced to learn as part of a puzzle!) how to use a real-world product while in-game.

FUTURE OUTLOOK

Across all gaming platforms, because of increased processing performance, new user interfaces are likely to emerge. Beyond the usual keyboard, mouse, or gamepad, new modes of interaction with games will probably include voice, sketch, gesture, touch, and force feedback. There will also be improvements in on-screen visual user interfaces as well as related audio cues.

By 2011, games connectivity will have become truly ubiquitous, and there are multiple ways in which game developers and gamers will exploit that connectivity. It seems certain that the games industry will fuel and drive that trend, creating new, exciting, and profitable online applications.

We see the emergence of tournament gaming, with experts competing while others observe online, as an interesting pointer to what may lie ahead.

We also see a trend in some blurring between actual sport (in the real world) and online sport. Telemetry data from NASCAR races are fed directly to online gamers who will experience the actual race through the game in a manner impossible in reality. Similar opportunities exist for other sports when either live or replayed data is captured from actual events.

GOING PRO: ESPORTS, LEAGUES, AND MORE

We will increasingly see online gaming as a spectator sport. The "Cyberathlete Professional League," founded in 1997, with sponsorship from nVIDIA, is today offering prize money of one million US dollars in its 2005 world tour.[14]

With virtual game environments quickly approaching visual levels of quality that 10 years ago were only found in expensive Hollywood special effects labs, the visual appeal of watching team matches in an immersive and visually appealing virtual environment may come to rival the appeal of watching people play tennis or soccer.

There are already TV channels—for example, GigaGames in Germany—devoted to a large extent to gaming content.

And betting on the results of major e-Sports tournaments has started in several locations, and special Web sites provide statistics and rankings on both individual players and teams.[15]

---

14. "NVIDIA to Sponsor $1,000,000 Cyberathlete World Tour," Press Release nVIDIA, February 3, 2005. www.nvidia.com/object/IO_18318.html.

15. Csports.net Clan Rankings, 2005. www.csports.net/TopClans.aspx.

BACK TO BUSINESS

Game technology and methods can be used for things other than gaming. It is likely that businesses may use technologies and methods developed in multiplayer games to facilitate virtual-team communication across a diverse, mobile workforce.

One of the key problems with the increasingly mobile knowledge worker is the absence of physical "shared spaces." Telephone conferences and document sharing may not transmit the same level of trust you could feel in a physical location. However, trust and a feeling of belonging to a group are something that has been shown to develop in MMOG environments, despite people never having seen each other.

It would not be the first time that innovation in virtual collaboration would take place in the private or academic sector first, and then migrate toward businesses. For example, instant messaging— a technology laughed at even a few years ago as the realm of teenagers not knowing how to pass their time—has become a key real-time collaboration and knowledge sharing tool in multinational companies and allows the instant creation and disbanding of communities and virtual meetings.

FREE CONTENT AND OPEN SOURCE IN GAMES

Professor Eric von Hippel of MIT Sloan has done extensive research on the benefits of user-driven innovation.[16] In the gaming industry, we see two versions of this type of user-driven innovation:

- So-called Mods or Total Conversions, which use existing commercial game engines and affect major change to the game content (new levels, new characters, new items, and so on), going all the way to building a completely new game (including new music, new textures, and so forth).
- New games built from scratch, including the underlying game engine.

---

16. von Hippel, Eric,"Democratizing Innovation," MIT Press, Cambridge, MA, 2005.

MODDING AND TOTAL CONVERSIONS

A vibrant community of gamers has shown that they can add significant value with its creativity. Many publishers have embraced the modding (user-created enhancements and extensions of existing game engines) community and support modding by providing the level editing tools that were used to create the original game.

Some modifications (for example, *CounterStrike*, which innovated team-based first-person shooters) have become so successful that they were folded back into commercial versions then sold off the shelf. Often a successful modification increases the shelf-life of a commercial game, allowing a longer sales period of the aging game, as it is refreshed with new content.

While some publishers make outdated versions of their games available for free, this model still usually requires buying the underlying game engine in form of a packaged game—even if most or all of the original content and artwork is to be replaced with a Mod or Total Conversion.

NEW GAMES FROM SCRATCH

Another more recent trend is the creation of whole games (game engine and content) from scratch under an open source license. For example, the following games can be downloaded and modified for free:

- *FreeCiv*, a multi-player strategy game.[17]
- *Battle for Wesnoth*, a fantasy turn-based multiplayer strategy game.[18]
- *Planeshift*, an Open Source game that was developed from scratch, including the game engine.[19] The game engine is licensed under the GPL, whereas the artistic content is licensed under a more restrictive license.

---

17. www.freeciv.org.
18. www.wesnoth.org.
19. www.planeshift.it.

Just as a vibrant and profitable economy has developed around open source software, there are a number of conceivable business models around open source games, including the following:

- Operating servers with guaranteed uptime and preventing cheating.

- Providing assistance and managing the experience quality through game-masters.

- Taking a commission of items auctioned in-game against real money.

- Offering free play on a stable server that is paid for by in-game advertising.

STRATEGY ISSUES FOR THE GAMING INDUSTRY

The following sections describe some of the ongoing strategy implications for game publishers, content owners, ISPs, and access providers, advertisers, and device manufacturers.

GAME PUBLISHERS

The environment for games continues to change, and game developers and publishers need to grapple with the issues discussed in the following paragraphs.

CUSTOMER SUPPORT AND COMMUNITY MANAGEMENT

Game publishing used to be a "fire and forget" business model. After bugfixing had been done, companies often forget about the customer and concentrate on the next game.

However, with people investing increasing amounts of time and energy in a virtual environment, managing and supporting this community becomes a challenge all by itself. As Blizzard learned due to their *World of Warcraft* success, customer support headaches can be a side-effect of having a mass-market success on one's hands.[20]

---

20. Schiesel, Seth, "World of Warcraft Keeps Growing, Even as Players Test Its Limits," *The New York Times,* February, 10, 2005.

MARKET RESEARCH

As games become more and more expensive to produce, a flop in the marketplace can be disastrous for the publisher. Games will have to do more precise targeting and perhaps co-development with their customer communities to avoid expensive flops.

SEPARATION OF THE GAME ENGINE FROM CONTENT CREATION

A major concern in the games industry is the increasing cost of game development.

For new games titles, development costs are rising, almost in line with the increasing performance and capabilities of each new generation of games platforms. For the 2005-06-generation of games consoles, some estimates put the figure at $20 million per premier game title. As these costs rise, fewer and fewer games titles will be able to achieve sufficient sales volume to break even.

While the games industry may increasingly be compared to the movie makers of Hollywood, game developers still reinvent the base technology (the "game engine") for each new project, whereas nobody in Hollywood reinvents a movie camera each time they shoot a film.

As we move toward 2011, the games industry will need to look at containing the cost of game development. One lever toward this is the separation of games development itself from the development of tools for the games development process.

Such tools could be exclusively provided by a small number of companies specifically focused on that problem, or several developers could aggregate around a model by cooperating in using an open-source engine game physics engine while competing on the development of game content built on top of that engine (a so-called co-opetition model—cooperation and competition at the same time).

MODERN INTELLECTUAL PROPERTY LICENSES

Modding has become a way of having a community extend the useful lifetime (and thereby extending the sales and shelf-life and thereby profitability) of games. Content and brand owners will therefore need to walk a fine line between protecting their unique content and collaborating with the modding and open source communities—for example, by delineating clear rules for non-commercial or even commercial re-use.

Having explicit rules in place about what can and cannot be done with work based on commercial engines can avoid frictions between publishers and the communities of their heavy users.

The profitable partnership between commercial IT companies and the open source community has proven that a company does not need exclusive ownership of a piece of software to make money with it. A similar model can help game publishers lower their costs by tapping into the fan community for some aspects, while keeping other aspects proprietary.

Tapping into a license framework like Lawrence Lessig's "Creative Commons" licenses,[21] which can be used to define specific aspects like only non-commercial use, can be a way to do this.

CONTENT OWNERS

Content owners will have to shift toward more interactivity and even more specialised, premium-quality, and "hyperlocal" content to provide value to an audience that has exploding options of where to spend their attention—and that can obtain much of their content requirements for free.

This is not because it would be pirated, but because other people are making their content available—the podcasting boom in the audio arena is only a precursor to what can happen in the video arena.

Companies, like Google, already provide platforms for anyone to publish (and sell, if they like) their own video content.[22]

---

21. creativecommons.org.
22. Hu, Jim, "Google queues up video," CNET news.com, April 4, 2005. news.com/Google%20queues%20up%20video/2100-1025_3-5653879.html.

ISPS AND ACCESS PROVIDERS

In a time when Internet access is being commoditized, ISPs and Access Providers can use multiplayer games to sell differentiated, premium access products to gamers willing to spend money on connectivity to make sure that it does not limit their gaming experience.

Although low-cost no-frills access providers are publicly criticised by state-of-the-art gamers, there seems to be a market for "Quality Brands" that cater to gamers and perhaps also other low-latency, high-bandwidth market sections.

ADVERTISERS

Advertisers need to become aware that an important part of their target audience is moving away from passive consumption media like TV or radio, toward interactive media.[23]

Advertisers need to forge new alliances with games publishers to provide product placement and other forms of advertising within the game context itself, as well as the community-driven interaction outside the game context. This is already beginning in mass-market games like *Splinter Cell*, and specialised agencies are starting to form around this market.

Online games have two additional attractive properties:

- They are very sticky due to the social networks that players build, as well as the investments in building up their character.
- They allow tracking of advertising exposure.

The question for advertisers is: Why not sponsor certain items in the game? Admittedly, fantasy games may not lend themselves very well to this, but the increasing number of games set in the present or near-future here could have a soft drink company

---

23. IBM Medienstudie 2005, IBM Business Consulting Services & ZEM Bonn University.

providing strength refills, a computer company providing in-games hardware or upgrades, and so forth.

Agencies that specialise in product placement for movies should have a look at diversifying into games and building up capabilities of tracking exposure in real time.

DEVICE MANUFACTURERS

Device manufacturers need to be innovative and creative for supporting games. Future game devices might not look at all like the current game devices.

Sony's Playstation Portable is already demonstrating that the mobile gaming device of the future will be not just dedicated gaming hardware. By providing MP3 and video capabilities, the Playstation Portable is truly turning into a mobile *entertainment* device.

CONCLUSION

The gaming industry, like other creative industries, taps the human imagination. The film industry, music publishing, and the book publishing industries are ones that also draw on the deep wells of the human spirit for creativity, fun, and surprises.

And if it's one thing that the history of those other creative industries show us, it's that they can make abrupt twists and turns. While many of the less imaginative will try to imitate the latest hit film, hit song, or hit book, the creative spirit is not an imitator. The human imagination is a big place, and there is plenty of room for many clever surprises to come.

We expect that the gaming industry will continue to thrive and will achieve things that we can't yet imagine.

7

The Soul of the Next Generation of Consumer Electronics Products

Lisa Su, Jim Kahle, Kevin Reardon, Allan Henderson

The Cell Broadband Engine (Cell BE) is a new processor chip jointly developed by IBM, Sony, and Toshiba that delivers the next leap in raw computing power. It is also the betting favorite to be the spark for the next consumer electronics (CE) revolution.

The Cell BE processor is sometimes called a "supercomputer on a chip" because it contains technical attributes from supercomputers, servers, and real-time systems and because a Cell BE processor runs media and high-performance workloads more than 10 times faster (on some applications) than today's PC configurations and for some key applications, many more times that speed.

Innovation drives the consumer electronics industry—new products, new features for existing products, new technologies, new services, and solutions are all part of the fuel that makes the CE industry hum. The Cell BE will enable many innovative products that will accelerate changes in the way we work, the way we play, and the way we interact with each other. The Cell BE processor is a key enabler of the long expected convergence of the computer, consumer, and network spaces in the market.

Shock waves are going through the entire industry, because the new processor is achieving such a leap in performance, while at the same time, doing it at a potentially low cost. The Cell BE will be able to play across a wide range of CE products, the first of which is the next generation of Sony Playstation.

In this chapter, we discuss what the Cell BE processor is, what it might mean to new, innovative products and applications, and what it might mean to the dynamics of the electronics industry as a whole.

WHAT IS THE CELL BE PROCESSOR?

The Cell BE processor has been shown to be at least 10 times faster than other microprocessors in applications like decryption, video decoding, and others—that is, in the sort of things you need to do in today's video-oriented consumer electronics.

Don't think the Cell BE will only be inside game machines. Cell BE processors provide lots of computing power that can easily handle all kinds of rich media applications, especially those applications that use broadband content. We're talking about computer games, movies, music, and anything else that uses large amounts of digital data or that needs to do lots of calculations in real time.

A Cell BE is designed to enable and accelerate most computing applications, including the ever more pervasive embedded applications in your TV, gaming systems, home server, and other essential interactive devices in our world today. You won't always see it, but you'll feel its impact.

And that includes the killer products that no one has thought about yet but that the blazing processor speed will make possible.

The Cell BE processor is a multi-core processor that's designed to handle a large number of tasks simultaneously. Traditionally, computer chips have had a single processor on one piece of silicon—in the same way most cars have a single engine. But the Cell BE has nine processor units called "cores" on a single silicon chip, the most of any commercial chip today (see Figure 7.1 for the architecture). (Other chip manufacturers are just starting to release multi-core processors with two cores.) Just think if your car had nine engines, each engine was as powerful as the single one you have today, and all nine fit in the same space under the hood.

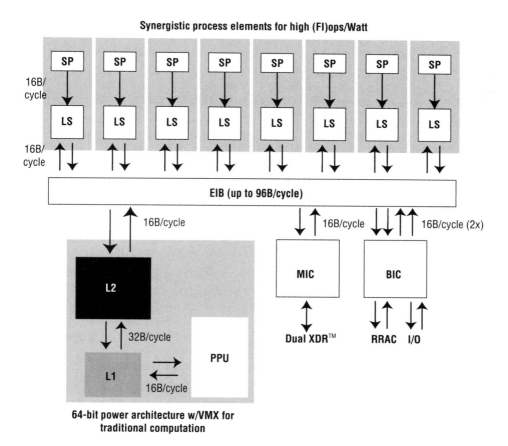

Figure 7.1   The first generation Cell BE processor.

A Cell BE processor has one 64-bit Power processor core that is the main processor and that also acts as the "conductor" for the flow of work to the others. Those other eight processors are "accelerator" processors, called synergistic processor elements (SPEs), each capable of general purpose computing in addition to massive floating point processing. A CBE with nine cores is called a 1+8 configuration.

CBE is a scalable architecture: You can scale down or scale up from 1+8. For applications that don't need as much performance, a product manufacturer can scale down by using CBE with fewer than eight synergistic processors. Or in large systems, several 1+8 CBEs can be linked into a larger coordinated system.

Besides the impressive leap in power, the Cell BE processor also represents an impressive leap in processor flexibility and richness of features. A great deal of advanced processor attributes are built into the Cell BE, which make it very flexible and able to be used in many different kinds of applications.

In fact, the flexibility of the Cell BE processor is almost as important as the fact that it works at ultra-high speeds.

HERE COMES THE CELL BE PROCESSOR

It took nearly five years, 300 engineers, and over $400 million to develop the Cell BE. The result is a very fast, very flexible, and ground-breaking processor chip, code-named "Cell" during its four plus year joint development because chips based on its architecture will be able to interoperate with one another as a single large system, inspired by the brain's network.

A typical game processor can usually be expected to ship somewhere in the neighbourhood of 10–20 million units a year. The expectations for the Cell BE processor are that it will be the heart of many other innovative consumer devices and so it could be shipping many times that number before too long.

SOME CELL BE PROCESSOR APPLICATIONS

If you are a product designer for an electronics company, what products do we expect that you will be able to make with an ultra-fast processor like the Cell BE processor? Let us explore some applications we envision in the next few years:

- Computer games become more realistic with very smooth, very realistic video graphics. There will be little left to remind you that you are not actually inside the game you're playing.

- Better graphics and richer audio will enable the creation of immersive 3D interactive devices. New collaborative environments will emerge.

- Functionality will move into software that today needs to be burned into hardware. Few of us know where the functionality in our electronics devices really resides. But once it is software-based, a TV can simply be upgraded, or the home server can be fixed by downloading a software patch over the Internet.

- User interfaces for consumer devices will be based on voice and touch. The keyboard that requires letter-by-letter typing has always been a severe constraint to natural human-machine interaction. With an ultra-fast processor giving you the ability to process much more data in real time, we will see much more pervasive voice-activated and graphics-activated touch interfaces.[1]

- Everyday objects such as mobile phones and MP3 players will participate in "smart environments" as they have seemingly intelligent digital capabilities that can be networked together.

---

1. The IBM Shorthand-Aided Rapid Keyboarding (SHARK) text input is an example for such an innovation. www.alphaworks.ibm.com/tech/sharktext.

WHY THE CELL BE PROCESSOR WILL SPARK A REVOLUTION IN CONSUMER ELECTRONICS

Using processors in CE products is certainly not a new concept, as many consumer products have had processors as control devices for several years.

However, three big shifts are contributing to an expected explosion in processor usage in future consumer electronics products that are more functionally rich. These three shifts are:

- Global digital network connectivity.
- Interactive rich media content.
- Rapidly growing software functionality.

Taken separately, each of these three shifts will significantly affect the market. But when combined, they will revolutionise consumer product design, delivery, and support and open the door for a new wave of devices, services, and solutions driven by these new fast processors with their unparalleled power. How software functionality grows in consumer electronics is the focus of Chapter 10, "Software Development Strategies for Connected Consumer Electronics"—but what about the network and content?

The convergence of the IT industry with the communications industry and with the consumer industry is being discussed already for at least half a century. However, the full promise of what could be possible was held up for two reasons that are tightly linked to each other in a chicken-and-egg scenario: 1) a high-speed global network and 2) digital content to flow over that network.

Despite the overwhelming and unheard success of the Internet, the missing link in the high-speed global network was what industry people call the "last mile"—or high-speed connection to the home. Even until recently, very few homes actually had high-speed connections, which made viewing video or listening to audio cumbersome.

In addition, debates over digital rights management (DRM) delayed acceptance of digital storage devices designed for its distribution, DVD, and consumer's willingness to make the investment in high-speed networks. As some elements of the DRM issues have been worked out (with the enhanced phone services such as DSL, Internet access over cable, and new wireless capabilities), the barriers of the "last mile" have begun to fall. Consumer acceptance of and desire for high-speed network connection to the home is rapidly growing, fuelling new processing and network demands. As digital TV and voice-over-IP replace their analogue equivalents and global standards emerge, very soon a totally new capability for communicating and interaction with content will be available around the world.

This is going to change the perspective on how to deal with this new world. If they are an infrastructure maker, they have to realize that everyone has very high-performance access devices now, so they need an infrastructure to support that. If they are a device maker, they have to realize that it's a given that high-speed computational functions and high-resolution graphics rendering are an expectation, not a novelty. And much more will need to change as well—the tools, the simulations, the content, and so forth. All this requires rethinking and redesign of further elements like the computing model, the architecture, and the user interaction.

COMPUTING MODEL

Another key element that will be new in the CE environment is the computing model (or operating system model). In the PC era, the programs and applications were primarily dependent on a single operating system—Windows.

With the advent of open source software like Linux and other technology, the PC model is unlikely to be repeated in the new digital CE space. The democracy and diversity of these will give CE consumers new flexibility and choices and radically accelerate innovation.

FLEXIBLE ARCHITECTURES

Just as the PC computing model must and will change, so too will we see changes in the PC's one-size-fits-all processor model. In the past, the scalability of the PC processor model was limited to accommodations for low-power or low-functionality and did not facilitate unique application optimization or special features, unless they were accepted en mass. However, embedded applications in CE will require a flexible architecture like the Cell BE processor that can be readily adapted to a particular purpose by a chip maker. The Cell BE is designed so that it can be opened up in a way few other processors have been.

USER INTERACTION

Looking ahead as the digital CE world evolves, new human interfaces and new technologies will radically change how people interact with CE devices, unencumbered by the PC legacy and limitations. As devices are designed for use in CE applications, consumers will expect devices they can intuitively interact with. This will drive more touch-screen type devices, newer physical interaction concepts, and more voice interactive devices. What this means is that we have opportunity to create new, intuitive user interfaces and new open standards for a new class of consumer devices that could happen in a way that's much different than the last time around—and that's where the growth is going to be.

REVOLUTION OR EVOLUTION?

A coming CE revolution is very exciting to think about, but we are still some steps away from such a revolution taking everything by storm.

Until we get the high-speed network proliferated everywhere so that consumers can get any high-speed interactive device connected no matter where they are and get access to the content they own and want, and until CE companies start creating the new high-function devices that the Cell BE processor will make possible, the revolution will remain an evolution, and consumers will still be on the uphill side of what is to come.

But we're going to see some radical changes in the second half of this decade. And the times in the market in 2010 and beyond will be absolutely thrilling.

SOME MORE ABOUT THE CAPABILITIES OF THE CELL BE PROCESSOR

In the following sections, we take a more detailed look at capabilities of the Cell BE processor that give those who are interested from a technical perspective a glimpse of what else is possible.

MORE THAN ONE PROCESSOR OR A CHIP FORM A MULTICORE ARCHITECTURE

Each of the several processors is called a "core," each of which can work independently but still stay coordinated—so that the system can be working on many applications or a single application at a given time. Think of it as something like putting more than one engine in your car. In general, multicore designs offer the performance of multiple processors but cost less, take up less space, and consume less power than designs with single cores.

Many chip manufacturers today are architecting two- or four-core designs. But the Cell BE processor has taken a giant stride to nine "cores" on a chip. There is one main 64-bit core that works together with eight "accelerator" cores, called synergistic cores, each capable of massive floating point processing. The 64-bit main processor core is based on the proven IBM Power Architecture™ and acts as the "conductor" among the other cores. These synergistic cores are called Synergistic Processing Elements (SPEs). From a performance and capability point of view, each SPE is comparable to a typical processor today.

It's important to note that the Cell BE has a myriad of other architectural attributes, from servers to real-time systems, which are at the leading edge and not found together in any other commercial chip.

THE MULTICORE ARCHITECTURE SPEED BOOST

Each of the eight synergistic cores can run a separate application thread, and the main core uses multi-threading to be able to run two threads. A thread is a single sequence of instructions executed in parallel with other threads. If a computer is a juggler, then each thread is an additional ball that the juggler keeps in the air in parallel.

So in a general sense, the Cell BE processor has $8 + 2 = 10$ threads running at the same time in parallel.

But we've actually written applications that get much more than a factor of 10 speed-up:

■   We have written demo programs with extra care to exploit the parallelism supported by the architecture. One demo program is an airplane flying through 3D images created from actual digitized geographical data. The demo flies through the data in real time, rendering smooth-motion graphics with ray casting techniques. It looks like you're flying through a real-world video, only sharper. With this demo, we're rendering 50x faster than we could do with today's 970 PowerPC® 970 processor.

■   And we have a Fast Fourier transform demo that's working at 100x speed-up. Fourier transforms are the basis of Digital Signal Processing (DSP) applications, including the conversion of analogue audio and video signals into digital form.

THE CHALLENGE TO PROGRAM IN PARALLEL

Parallel programming is often viewed as complex, but we worked closely with the software experts of the design team to make this relatively easy to program. Game programmers, accustomed to needing to code in assembly language are going to say, "Wow, I can use a compiler and still get more flexibility, much better performance, and more application power."

Our experience is that programming the Cell BE processor is not quite as easy as general purpose machines, but it's really not very hard once your mind shifts to thinking in a parallel paradigm. By analogy, think of playing the piano with one hand and then think of playing with two hands, each performing independent parts.

Very few people can do it well immediately, but very few people fail at it after a little practice.

Language compilers for a Cell BE (for C, C++, and so on) will be released, as open source, so that this community of innovative programmers can extend the programming capabilities and make it even easier. Its acceptance by the open source community will be one of the ultimate success factors for the Cell BE processor.

If they need to get an application going quickly, programmers will find that they will get performance improvements with minimal reprogramming.

But if they need to accelerate the application and take advantage of the parallelism that becomes possible, they will need to think a little harder. The CBE gives the programmer the ability to put processes on different SPEs so that they run in parallel. A programmer can create a great deal of parallelism across these eight accelerators.

But the Cell BE processor also lets the programmer parallelize memory moves. It is the first of its kind to be architected with a set of smart memory access engines in the chip that can multiply the parallelism by a factor of two. (These memory engines are direct memory access (DMA), which is a technique of transferring data from one memory area to another without having to go through the central processing unit.) Some engineers like to say that there are almost eight times two accelerators in a CBE: There's the eight regular ones that do the processing, and then there are eight smart DMA engines, to give you a total of 18 parallel engines.

In addition, many programmers have been doing that in symmetric multi-processing for a while now. What's different here is that the data movements are also parallel, so there's a new level of parallel thinking that can happen for better application performance and flexibility.

And the extra effort the software engineer put in is rewarded by large factors of performance improvements.

ARCHITECTURE INNOVATION

The Cell BE takes advantage of IBM's most advanced semiconductor process technologies to deliver high performance while consuming small quantities of power, which lets Cell BE processors be used in small devices in additional to more traditional computing machines. The design has built-in supercomputer attributes, like having accelerators, and also uses a full 64-bit architecture throughout. The designers took things from the high end and also learned things from embedded devices, like how to control memory, and then they innovated by using them together.

CBE designers took a holistic approach to architecting the Cell BE processor. The trick was that while they used a blank sheet to architect the chip, they did it within the overall framework of Power architecture, so they could reuse many existing pieces of intellectual capital used in the Power architecture.

Some other key Cell BE processor attributes include the following.

DESIGNING FOR INNOVATIVE MEMORY HANDLING

One of the really important things is how we move memory around. We have introduced a new memory structure into the architecture called the "local store," which resides in the SPE. It's a place to have software-controlled data movement in the chip. This is a novel feature used to allow parallel memory access in addition to parallel processing to support streaming models.

DESIGNING FOR LOW POWER USAGE

The amount of power the Cell BE processor uses is a key factor in the use of the CBE in consumer devices. Remember that many consumer devices are expected to run in your living spaces. If you're given X watts to drive a chip, you can't make the chip twice as big because then you'd need twice as much power. So you need to turn to efficiency. We constructed the SPEs so that they are two to four times more efficient than a standard general-purpose processor—so we can get that much more work done with the same amount of power. Also small quantities of power means that you generate less heat, and this heat reduction makes it effective to use the Cell BE processor in embedded applications.

VIRTUALIZATION TO ALLOW FOR MULTIPLE APPLICATIONS

The designers borrowed and extended the hypervisor technology used in high-end IBM systems. This is the virtualization technology inside the chip system, where you virtualize things to make smaller virtual systems. The CBE designers took it in a different direction, however, and used it to virtualize the Cell BE processor so that part of the chip can be used for real-time applications and part of the chip can be used for more traditional applications. So you can think of it as being able to be carved up to do completely different tasks that won't interfere with each other. For example, the Cell BE processor is capable of supporting multiple operating systems simultaneously. Those systems could include Linux, real-time operating systems for computer entertainment, and consumer electronics applications, as well as guest operating systems for specific applications.

OPTIMIZING FOR REAL TIME

The Cell BE processor has real-time controls running throughout the chip. The designers wanted to be sure they had all the hardware mechanisms needed to run a good real-time system. In a desktop computer, as one small example, you push a button and the computer tries to get to you as soon as it can. However, in gaming systems and other real-time systems, you need instantaneous attention.

BUILT-IN SECURITY CAPABILITIES

SPEs can be put into a security mode so that you can have a virtual trusted computing platform. This provides the capability of checking that the user is authenticated to use certain content.

The bottom line is that other chip manufacturers brag about a single new, innovative feature in their chip design. But there are dozens of ground-breaking features throughout the architecture of the CBE, and it's probably going to take people a little while to find them all and then exploit them. The Cell BE processor really takes things to a new level.

HOW TO MAKE A CLEAN DESIGN

It's true that backward compatibility is always important. There's always a large installed base of applications that is for good business reasons you don't want to abandon. And when you make only small, incremental performance improvements, as has traditionally been the case, then a strict evolutionary path is your only option; it's hard to get out of the box.

However, when you have a large enough leap in performance, and 10x is a pretty large leap, then you can take care of backward compatibility with emulation.

HOW DOES THE CELL BE PROCESSOR SCALE?

Think of the typical Cell BE processor as the 1+8 configuration, which is the configuration that is first going to be release and the configuration that is going to be used in the next generation Playstation from Sony. There is one main core, plus eight synergistic cores. That's the 1+8 basic cell.

But the Cell BE processor is architected to make it relatively easy to manufacture scaled down cells that have fewer than eight synergistic processors. Possible configurations include 1+4 and 1+2. You can see from looking at a picture of the CBE that it looks very regular. The Cell BE processor was designed to be very modular so that you can change the number of SPEs with relative ease. The designers worked very hard to make a modular design so that it would be physically easy to change the configuration compared to customizing other chip architectures.

Or you can scale up the Cell BE processor by linking together several 1+8 cells into a larger coordinated system. You can configure two, four, or sixteen cells to work together into a super system. As the designers thought about scaling up, the Cell BE processor was designed so that two cells could be coupled together without having to make any changes to the processor itself or add any new chips. The I/O system of the CBE can be used to connect to an I/O chip or to connect to another Cell BE processor. All the flexibility is already built into the chip to allow scaled-up configurations.

The design thinking at this time is that applications that need to use more than two cells will probably go into cluster configurations that use large numbers of chips connected together, much like large clusters are today.

GENERAL- OR SPECIAL-PURPOSE?

The Cell BE processor is a general-purpose computer that excels at parallel processing and real-time processing. It has been optimized to drive the new generation of consumer devices, but that doesn't exclude it from being used elsewhere.

Each of the SPEs is a general-purpose processor in itself, and each is completely programmable, so you can generate a great deal of parallelism.

There is also a lot of flexibility in the Cell BE processor, much more than you see with standard vector machines or with super-computers—in fact, much more than anything else.

CONCLUSION

The Cell BE processor today is just starting to drive a handful of consumer products: the next Sony Playstation or high-definition digital TVs from Toshiba and Sony. But you can expect the ultra-fast Cell BE processors to start quickly appearing in more and more consumer devices.

You can bet that in the near future, the Cell BE processor will fuel even more innovative consumer products, which are the lifeblood of the CE industry.

But the upcoming CBE based products, when combined with the coming global digital network connectivity, with the dramatic increase in interactive rich media content, and with rapidly growing software functionality, will lead to thrilling times for the consumer electronics industry. And it will lead to lucrative times for those companies like Sony, Toshiba, and IBM that are poised to capitalize on these new industry developments.

IBM's Global Technology Outlook and Its Implications to Consumer Electronics

Iris Ginzburg, Akihiro Horibe, Yossi Lichtenstein, Norishige Morimoto, Robin Williams

Innovation is the lifeblood of the electronics industry. It pulses with new ideas and new products such as FAX, the PC, the MP3 player, the mobile phone, and many infrastructure innovations, some of which fundamentally change the way people live, work, and play. Innovation occurs at the intersection of invention and business insight—in a fusion of new developments and new approaches to solve problems.

IBM uses its Global Technology Outlook (GTO) process to systematically gain insight about the future of technology, to identify trends, and to project where the next inventions and innovations may occur. IBM has used this process and the previous ten-year outlook now for more then 20 years, and it has proven to be very useful. Allowances, however, need to be made for breakthrough, especially when extrapolating technology development, because it does sometimes miss predicting disruptive technologies like the World Wide Web phenomenon, which caused a fundamental shift in the way we now do business.

HOW THE GLOBAL TECHNOLOGY OUTLOOK IS PREPARED

IBM's research division conducts an annual GTO in addition to, but often feeding into, its ongoing cycle of strategy and planning. The process starts in March each year by them selecting a core production team and representatives from each of IBM's eight Research labs to work on it. A call for topics is issued to the IBM research community, which is the largest and most prolific IT industrial research community in the world and which is largely responsible for IBM receiving the most US patents (a record 3,248 in 2004) already for the twelfth consecutive year.

The call for GTO topics typically generates about 100 topics that are related to IBM's current or future businesses opportunities. They have a technical basis and cover a timeframe of about three to five years, although some technology topics may look further ahead. The topics include technology and business trends and disruptive changes that people think are likely to happen. They are all presented to the core team, lab representatives, and the research senior vice president. Similar ideas are clustered into single topics, and the best of them all are selected for further studies.

Teams of researchers then work on the selected topics, further refining and consolidating them. External opinions are also sought, and more analysis is performed as vice presidents of the research division take ownership of the topics in their areas.

Five to 10 topics are finalized by the core headquarters team as the GTO for the year, and an IBM-confidential presentation is given to IBM's chairman and other top executives in December. A non-confidential GTO and some industry oriented versions are created and subsequently presented to customers to share IBM's view of the future with them. The GTO is a popular presentation in meetings with customers where IBM discusses customer-specific problems and possible IBM solutions, which is generally received with very good feedback.

In the following sections, we present selected topics from the 2004 and 2005 GTOs and describe the implications to consumer electronics for each of them. These include the following:

- Hardware technology
- People proxies
- Speech technology
- Security and privacy
- Connectivity

HARDWARE TECHNOLOGY AND SYSTEMS

The first and most detailed topic of the GTO is always a survey of hardware technology trends and outlooks. This reflects IBM's history as well as the continued central position of hardware technology in IBM's research division.

Our main outlook messages for hardware are that the semiconductor industry is entering a new era of uncertainty and risk and that cycle time between technology generations will increase.

Before discussing risk, however, let us share the optimistic long-term view of hardware technology: The hardware growth rate will continue to increase! As each generation of technology reaches its limitations, new breakthroughs will continue to be found to increase that progress again.

In particular, integrated circuit technology based on silicon transistors has delivered almost seven orders of magnitude of performance improvement in the last half century. More is still expected.

As an illustration, compare supercomputers and brains. Various types of estimates are used to compare brain operations to computer calculations—for example, the density of retinal cells extrapolated up to the volume of the brain. IBM's Deep Blue supercomputer from 1997 is comparable to the computing power of a lizard brain, while by 2015, a supercomputer will have the power of a human brain. Five to 10 years later, this power will be at the desktop and in the living room. Thus we can say that computational power growth in about two decades will correspond to hundreds of millions of years of evolution.

Now let us turn to the more sober mid-term outlook, which can be summarized as the following:

- Power dissipation, parameter variability, and new packaging to cater to performance and bandwidth requirements at the chip level.

- Accelerators and integrated system design for performance at the system level.

CHIP-LEVEL TRENDS

The first issue is that passive power, or leakage, is growing faster than active transistor-switching power. Due to cooling limitations in high-end processors with several hundred million transistors, not all transistors can operate simultaneously at full speed. This trend will continue, and by 2010, only a fraction of the several billion transistors on a chip will be usable at any particular moment in time. Advanced cooling technologies, such as liquid cooling, will be needed to address this overheating problem. Another direction is that future systems will need to dynamically manage power at runtime by turning system elements on and off and by controlling operation frequencies.

A second chip-level issue deals with the variability in chip functionality and manufacturing yield. Parameter variability comes from physical effects—for example, the variable thickness of gate oxide, as well as process variability such as the effects of temperature changeability on yield. Like passive power, this variability issue will limit performance, and future designs will need to take it into consideration.

A review of trends in the chip-level packaging and interconnection of electronic chips leads to interesting insight. The main drivers are performance and the ever larger need for inter-chip bandwidth.

High-end chips are already packaged in plastic, not ceramics; soon, chip stacking will be commonly used, and in five to 10 years, 3D silicon integration will be state of the art. Although these new packaging techniques will provide more performance and bandwidth, their progress is not as predictable as the current integration and packaging technologies.

SYSTEM-LEVEL TRENDS

At the system level, hardware accelerators were historically outpaced by the rapid growth of processor frequency. For example, graphic accelerators included special-purpose hardware to process graphics much faster than general processors.

However, as the performance of general processors increased and their price decreased so rapidly, they outpaced the special-purpose, relatively expensive graphic processors at least for the general market. Now, as the progress of general processors is bound to decrease, system performance will increasingly rely on accelerators. Examples include an Intel® IO accelerator, an IBM cryptographic processor, a Cray computation accelerator, and IBM's Cell Broadband Engine processor designed to accelerate media processing and streaming workloads (see Chapter 7, "The Soul of the Next Generation of Consumer Electronics Products," for a detailed discussion of the Cell BE).

Finally, there is the integration over the entire computational stack, from semiconductor technology to end-user applications. This stack integration will replace processor frequency as the major driver of increased system performance. In particular, systems will be designed to dynamically manage and optimize power and to use multi-processors, accelerators, and other modular components for continued performance leadership.

MAIN TREND

The main mid-term implication for the consumer electronics industry is that it should anticipate computational performance increase, but possibly not at an as quick and predictable pace as before. At the same time, systems will become more complex and will require better and new skills to build consumer applications upon them.

In the long-term (that is, in about 15 years), super-computing power will be available to the end-consumer. This availability of super-computing power will surely open a large variety of opportunities from virtual reality to consumer optimization. Forecasting for this, however, is both difficult and beyond the scope of this book.

THE EMERGENCE OF PEOPLE PROXIES

Last year's GTO already predicted that a new wave of productivity will rise as people and business processes get more closely aligned (see Figure 8.1).

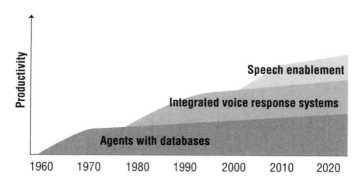

Figure 8.1   Organizational productivity grows through people and business alignment.

According to this theme, enterprises hold abundant information about people—both employees and customers. However, this information is scattered in many disparate databases and lacks integration. A federated, digital representation of people will emerge, called the Person Proxy. This Person Proxy will dynamically and automatically capture increasingly rich information about individuals. Such proxies will become first-class programming constructs that enable automation and optimization of business processes resulting in substantial productivity gains for individuals and the enterprise.

Another claim is that applications for People Proxies will produce value both to individuals and to the enterprise. For example, datamining for enterprise skill assessment could answer the question of how many people have Web services development experience. Currently, people must provide data about their jobs, skills, and experience manually. But in the future, the automated capture of this expertise, for example, from project documents—will make proxies more accurate and complete. Individuals will benefit from personalized e-learning, which automatically matches content to skills and experience, availability, free time, and location. And as a combination of enterprise and individual value—contextual collaboration will use accurate expertise, role, and availability information to dynamically locate the right people at the right time to collaborate on a task.

Although the focus here is on People Proxies in the enterprise context, there are also immediate implications for consumer electronics. As customers are to be represented by proxies, CRM, loyalty programs, and e-commerce will evolve to make use of People Proxies.

Long-term implications of People Proxies may relate to CE products that will dynamically customize their functionality to their customers.

PERVASIVE CONNECTIVITY

The next topic is the dramatic effect on network volume and traffic patterns through the massive deployment of smart and networked sensors.

Large amounts of data, such as automatically generated sensor data, voice, and multimedia data will be carried over heterogeneous physical networks running the Internet protocol. The ratio of client to server data will increase from 1 to 50 today to 100 to 1 in the future.

This pervasive, broadband connectivity will enable new applications and services across every industry sector. For example, industries will need to re-invent IT infrastructures to benefit from networked RFID[1] and smart sensors. Consider car-making as an example: Components for the car are procured from many vendors around the world, but component defects result in very expensive recalls for the car manufacturer. RFID will be utilized to automate component tracking and should result in better procedures for handling defects, reducing costs, and improving customer satisfaction.

The dramatic change in the location of data generation, its volume, and traffic patterns will be a paradigm shift toward aggregation and management of data locally. In other words, data will be managed at the edge of the network. The Internet protocol will be augmented to provide the semantics and application layer information required for intelligent routing. And there will be many opportunities for middleware and services to filter and analyze data in an intelligent manner.

Pervasive connectivity will require additional care regarding security and privacy. These concerns will grow driving new hardware and software solutions for data management, access control, and user authentication.

As for implications for consumer electronics, pervasive connectivity may bring new features and totally new ideas to many CE products. We mentioned earlier the implications for electronics manufacturing.

SPEAK TO IT

The 2005 GTO predicts that speech technology is becoming a critical enabler for a holistic customer experience.

---

1. Radio Frequency Identification is the technology used for tags on items in warehouses, shops, ID cards, and so on. RFID has the advantage of very cheap tags.

Customer demand for choice, convenience, and consistency across interaction channels will drive integration of voice-based and Web-based business processes. On the technology front, a leap in voice technology has recently enabled many successful deployments with reusable speech components that will greatly accelerate cost-effective deployments in the near future (see Figure 8.2 for that productivity enhancement).

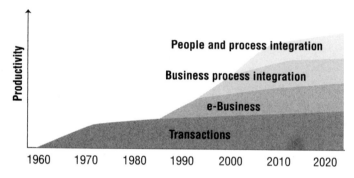

Figure 8.2   Productivity enhancements in call centers.

Take this concrete example of speech enablement in call centers. The cost of a single transaction with a human agent is between $4 to $9, while an automated transaction costs between 25 and 45 cents. This dramatic decrease in cost can result in large savings. Assuming a volume of 100 million calls, which is typical in financial services call centers, going from 50 to 60 percent automation saves $45 million, or 16 percent of expenses. In addition, studies show considerable reduction in caller interaction time and also a boost to staff morale.

As to the technology, base speech recognition has improved steadily over the last 15 years, and current error rates are low enough for many practical applications. Voice user interfaces mimic graphical user interfaces with standard interaction models that include a toolbar of spoken universals, consistency of dialog strategies and metaphors, and context settings. Users are empowered by menus, free-form dialogs, context-sensitive help, correction, navigation, shortcuts, and hints. Implementation has become cost effective with reusable speech solution modules that include all the dialogues, grammars, and call flows needed to obtain units of information. These modules can be composed into larger units and embedded into multiple applications.

The mid-term implications for the CE industry are clear: Speech technology will revolutionize the way companies interact with their customers. Longer-term it seems plausible to have consumer electronics devices that can listen and react.

LEGISLATION AND DATA

Recent security and business incidents have made governments and industry groups anxious to regulate how data is to be compiled, managed, protected, shared, used, and retained. As a result, enterprises have to change their processes to ensure compliance and avoid disruptions. Enterprise and IT industry response to new legislation will be costly, but it opens opportunities for legislative compliance products and services.

In the short-term, many kinds of products and services will be introduced for compliance, reporting, and data. Common tools will emerge in the mid-term to analyze and verify compliance and risk management. Afterwards, architected frameworks will emerge to enable rapid response and a separation of compliance procedures from business processes.

The implications of these regulation trends for the CE industry seem mostly negative. The implementation of compliance systems will drain resources from more desirable projects. On the positive side, IT will evolve from addressing specific regulatory requirements to architectural solutions, which will establish flexible and robust IT architectures.

ADDITIONAL THEMES

The 2004 and 2005 Global Technology Outlooks include many other interesting themes, including the following.

STOCHASTIC ANALYSIS AND OPTIMIZATION

Stochastic methods capture the variability within systems as well as environmental uncertainty. Capturing the effects of variability is increasingly important because decisions are required more frequently, robustness is critical for the operations, and deterministic approximations are inadequate for complex systems. At the same time, advances in computational speed, algorithms, and the availability of data are creating new opportunities to exploit sophisticated stochastic methods.

For consumer electronics, as for other industries, these methods will improve the robustness of operations and our understanding of markets and other complex systems.

ON-DEMAND WORLD

Businesses will increasingly need the ability to dynamically respond to changes in the business environment, understand and control complex dynamics and collective behavior, and manage large volumes of sensitive data on heterogeneous interconnected systems. A fundamentally new "on-demand" approach is needed for these challenges, bringing opportunities in modeling, optimization, security, and trust creation techniques forward.

THE ARCHITECTURE OF BUSINESS

Businesses are componentizing into discrete services to achieve operational efficiency, flexibility, and to sharpen their focus. At the same time, Web services will accelerate the move toward service-oriented architectures.

These trends will converge to enable formal modeling of businesses and the structured linkage between businesses and IT to efficiently deploy, monitor, and manage business operations in consumer electronics, as in other industries.

REVOLUTION IN ENTERPRISE SOFTWARE

Industry ecosystems are being transformed by networks of companies that provide business process components, standards, and solutions. Software as a service is an emerging alternative to buying or developing solutions.

In the near future, monolithic enterprise software development will give way to a new flexible, standards-based, service-oriented solution assembly approach.

METADATA

The explosion of data as well as the componentization of software and businesses is increasing the need for data about data, or metadata.

Metadata and search capabilities will be exploited to create new unexpected applications and business models. Metadata standards are already emerging across many industries, including consumer electronics, and they will accelerate interoperability across value nets.

CONCLUSION

Each of the themes we presented in this chapter has quite clear mid-term implications for the way consumer electronics businesses will be managed.

Long-term implications are, as usual, more difficult to predict, but as with the themes we have reviewed, we speculate that within approximately ten years, these technological trends will also be reflected in actual consumer electronics products.

Embedded Linux: For Embedded Systems Today and into the Future

Nobuhiro Asai

What do you sketch if someone asks you to draw a picture of a computer system? Do you draw a desktop computer or a laptop? Or do you draw a mobile phone or microwave oven? Most of us still imagine a computer system as looking like a monitor and keyboard-type computer that you can immediately recognize as being a computer. But the world has been changing.

Computers are fading into the other products, devices, and appliances that are all around us. Many believe that eventually computers will be all but invisible. They will be completely embedded in those other devices, with nothing left that looks like today's image of a computer.

EMBEDDED SYSTEMS

Such embedded systems are not new. Your microwave oven has a small computer system in it, as does your mobile phone. And your car has more embedded computers than you would think possible. An embedded system is a computer system that is completely encapsulated by the device it controls. Examples of products with embedded computer systems include Personal Digital Assistants (PDAs), mobile phones, Digital TV and set top box, home server, hub and router, and even a wrist watch.

But the newest embedded systems that are now coming out have dramatically improved capabilities and potential. And that's because the processing power of the chips that run these new embedded systems are much more powerful. It's also because the available memory can be much larger than in the older systems. And when you get increased processing power and memory, you have the potential for whole new applications and devices.

Why are people interested in embedded systems? It's because embedded systems represent a huge new business opportunity. Predictions are that the market for embedded systems will soon be larger than general purpose computing, eventually much larger. The world market for embedded systems is predicted to double from a little over $40 billion in 2004 to over $80 billion in 2009.[1] Current research also estimates that Embedded Linux revenues will reach $118.5 million by 2006, growing at a compound annual growth rate (CAGR) of 22 percent.[2]

The number of consumer devices using embedded computer systems will eventually outnumber PCs. As the devices proliferate and computing is embedded in new places, all kinds of new interactions and transactions become possible.

THE DEVELOPMENT OF CONSUMER ELECTRONICS AND SOME IMPLICATIONS TO EMBEDDED SYSTEMS

We see from Figure 9.1 that there are three evolutionary stages of Consumer Electronics: digitalization, networking, and platform-based, and embedded systems play across each of these stages.

1. Krishnan, Ravi, "G-229R Future of Embedded Systems Technology," bcc, June, 2005.
2. "22% growth rate forecast for Linux," CIMtalk, August 19, 2004, www.cimtalk.com/news/vdc/vdc102.html.

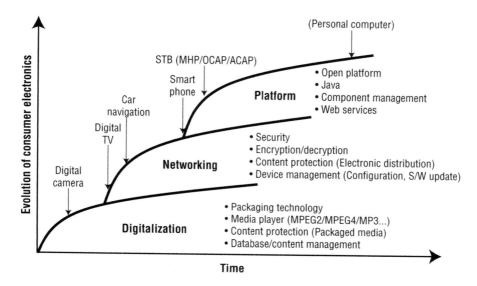

Figure 9.1 Evolution of consumer electronics.

1. The first step is the ability to handle digital content, which we call "digitalization" in the illustration. Digital content is provided as a packaged media like DVD/CD or from digital broadcasting. Digital content is transferred among devices by a recordable media or by attaching it as a network drive through USB. Most consumer electronics products are in this phase today (2005).

2. The second step is "networking." This is a huge step up from the digitalization phase given that devices need to interoperate with other unknown persons and devices through the Internet. Security functions become more important. Of course, security is not just for the integrity of software in the device; it includes data protection, privacy protection, and content protection. Interoperability is an essential requirement for networked consumer electronics devices.

3. The next step is "platform." In this phase, consumer electronics products become more "open" and able to accept downloadable software or services. You are not just downloading content, but you can download changes to the system itself.

Java is one of the key technologies for this open platform. The OSGi service platform defined by the OSGi Alliance[3] that manages life-cycle of software (installing, activating, de-activating, and uninstalling) plays a key role in this kind of component management (see Chapter 4, "The Smart Home: Coming to Your House Soon, but Not Too Soon," for more about OSGi platforms in the Smart Home).

The evolution of consumer electronics so far has been driven mostly by the first "digital content" phase. CE devices have incorporated the functions to handle digital contents, and they are becoming richer as the digital content improves to high-definition.

Most embedded systems up to the recent past have been fixed function devices with a single configuration of software. But the capabilities of embedded systems have significantly expanded, driven by the increase in computing capability that can be packed into a small amount of space. Because older embedded systems were limited in processing and memory, they were only capable of special purpose applications. But the embedded systems that are appearing today are much more powerful, and they can be built with general purpose hardware and a general purpose operating system, using the application code to shape the functionality of the product.

Most software components for special-purpose embedded systems were not very big or complex and thus could be developed in-house by the CE manufacturer. But as networking and platform support gains importance, software for these embedded systems is becoming more complex. And developing the software is a more complex task too, one that is unlikely to be done solely in-house by a consumer electronics manufacturer.

In the late 1990s, a majority of consumer electronics manufacturers in Japan had used ITRON (Industrial TRON[4]), a real-time operating system (RTOS) kernel designed by Professor Ken Sakamura

---

3. www.osgi.org.
4. TRON—"The Real-time Operating system Nucleus,"
   www.assoc.tron.org/eng/ and ITRON, www.sakamura-lab.org/TRON/
   ITRON/home-e.html.

from the University of Tokyo. The specification of ITRON is open to the public. Many chip vendors have implemented ITRON on their chip sets, and many CE manufacturers adopted ITRON for consumer electronics products. In North America, a variety of real-time operating systems like VxWorks[5] and pSOSystem[6] from Wind River or QNX Neutrino[7] had been used.

Around the year 2000, along with the evolution of hardware processor speed and memory size to handle digital contents and diversification of consumer needs, embedded systems required handling much more complex applications. The operating system of choice for this realm has become Embedded Linux—the real-time version of the vastly popular open source operating system, Linux.

The development cost for the software portion of a given product has been growing rapidly. To reduce this cost, the demand for an extensible RTOS with a variety of selectable components appeared. The emergence of open source projects and the associated concept for intellectual property protection of a "General Public License" (GPL) did not only have the widely discussed impact on the PC industry, but also found a lot of interest in the CE industry. Consumer electronics manufacturers need to incorporate many standards to be interoperable while at the same time differentiate themselves. Often, the organizations that govern those standards provide sample implementations of them. But to actually implement those standard functions within their products, those samples need to be ported to the proprietary operating system and be fully tested by the manufacturers themselves.

WHAT IS EMBEDDED LINUX?

Just like your desktop computer needs an operating system, an embedded system needs an operating system. The operating system of choice in the case of embedded systems is quickly becoming Embedded Linux.

5. www.windriver.com/products/device_technologies/os/vxworks6/.
6. www.windriver.com/products/device_technologies/os/psosystem_3/.
7. www.qnx.com/products/rtos/.

Embedded Linux is a dialect of the Linux, open source operating system used primarily on servers (and often on desktops, too). Linux is a highly regarded open source operating system and continues to evolve through contributions of the worldwide development community.

When you need an operating system that is powerful, reliable, flexible, and scalable, combined with extensive support for a multitude of microprocessor architectures, hardware devices, graphics, and communications protocols, you are looking at the strengths of the Linux operating system.

Used by millions in all industries, Linux is the world's fastest-growing operating system. And Embedded Linux is already being used today in PDAs, mobile phones, routers, MP3 players, set top boxes, and much more.

Just like other versions of Linux, Embedded Linux is open source. This means that it is built by the collaborative efforts of programmers around the world. No one owns Linux, unlike proprietary operating systems that are controlled by a single company that can decide what functionality is available, when it is available, and who has access to the interfaces to the functionality. Anyone can change Linux at the source code level.

To keep some order in what could be a wildly chaotic Linux environment (if everyone can change Linux, how can it be stable enough to use in a commercial product?), different groups create Linux distributions. These distributions are packages of code that make up a working Linux system. Some companies do that for profit. Some collaborative groups provide free distributions.

Some of the attributes of Linux that make it attractive for the use in embedded systems include the following:

- Linux is already a recognized standard as an operating system for computers—and especially for servers. This makes it the world's fastest proliferating operating system.
- Linux is renowned for its speed, reliability, and security, but especially that its open source code is developed and maintained by the Linux community.

- Linux continues to evolve through contributed efforts of the worldwide development community. Source code is available with few restrictions on use or requiring royalties, and there are many alternatives for getting working code as Linux is not single-sourced.

- Linux has powerful networking, interoperability, and security capabilities.

- Programmers are available in large numbers to develop product applications.

- Linux provides a stable, secure, and scalable system.

- Many standard components are available that can be applied to consumer electronics products.

Linux has already been used in development projects involving cash registers, wristwatches, and mobile phones. The TiVo digital video recorder, the Sony PlayStation, and the Sharp Zaurus all use Linux.

SMALL BUT MIGHTY: THE LINUX WATCH

IBM Research has significantly expanded the scope of Linux by demonstrating Linux running on a wristwatch.

Designed to communicate wirelessly with PCs, cell phones, and other wireless-enabled devices, the watch has the ability to display condensed email messages and directly receive pager-like messages in addition to calendar, address book, and to-do list functions.

ACHIEVING EMBEDDED LINUX PROGRESS: CONSORTIUMS

Open source means that anyone could change Linux and make his or her own version, but it is not in the interest of the parties to have their own personal dialect of Linux. What is important is the accumulated benefit of a community of clever programmers all collaborating to build a better Linux.

Because collaboration is the key to success, Linux consortiums and forums exist to act as collaboration hubs. Two key collaboration efforts for building a better Embedded Linux are the following:

- The Embedded Linux Consortium.
- The Consumer Electronics Linux Forum.

THE EMBEDDED LINUX CONSORTIUM

To respond to broad interests in using Linux for embedded devices, the Embedded Linux Consortium (ELC) was formed as a nonprofit and vendor-neutral trade association in 2000.

The ELC released the ELC Platform Specification (ELCPS) in 2003, defining standard application programming interfaces (API) for embedded applications to achieve the desired high degree of interoperability. The platform specification is intended to help unify the fragmented embedded marketplace. It enables software developers to work with different sets of APIs to develop one application to run on multiple devices. With the interfaces defined by the ELC, companies can develop applications without being tied to a single operating system.

Mid-2005, the primary objective of the ELC had been achieved and the ELCPS was transferred to the Open Source Development Labs (OSDL) for further development. At the same time, the ELC ceased to exist.[8]

The standard platform defines three system environments to be proper subsets of a Linux standard base (LSB), as follows:

- A minimal system environment for deeply embedded systems that have minimal or no user interfaces.
- An intermediate system environment that supports file systems, asynchronous I/O, and dynamic linking.

---

8. www.osdl.org/newsroom/press_releases/2005/
    2005_09_09_beaverton.html.

■ The full system environment for the broader spectrum of embedded devices, not intended specifically for consumer electronics products.

THE CONSUMER ELECTRONICS LINUX FORUM

In 2003, Matsushita, Sony, Hitachi, NEC, Philips, Samsung, Sharp, and Toshiba announced the formation of the Consumer Electronics Linux Forum (CE Linux Forum or CELF). Right after that announcement, IBM also joined the CE Linux Forum as an active participant.

The objectives of the CE Linux Forum are to formalize requirements for Linux extensions that meet the needs of consumer electronics products, develop patches to the main line Linux kernel in response to those requirements, and promote broader use of Linux for CE products.

As described earlier, the Embedded Linux Consortium is focusing on defining proper subsets of APIs for the interoperability of applications and middleware for wide range of embedded devices. In contrast, the CE Linux Forum looks solely after the consumer electronics space to solve immediate issues that might hinder the adoption of Embedded Linux in consumer electronics products.

Initially, the CE Linux Forum worked on the real-time capability; reduced boot-up time; enhanced audio, video, and graphic functions, a sophisticated power management; and minimized system size. To address those issues, five working groups were established right away with an additional one in place, looking swiftly after security topics.

The CE Linux Forum published its first specification and reference implementation in 2004 (both are freely available on the CE Linux Forum Web site[9]). This first release includes the output from the

---

9. www.celinuxforum.org.

six working groups, and the reference implementation incorporates nearly all of the functions defined in this initial specification.

After the successful release of an initial specification, the CE Linux Forum has extended its coverage to include middleware. Size and development cost of middleware within an entire software stack has grown rapidly, while at the same it is less of a differentiating component. Therefore, consumer electronics manufacturers start defining a set of middleware for a specific domain, pointing out related open source projects, and defining APIs for outside components to plug-in. As middleware often depends on the application domain of a CE product, vertically-oriented working groups were established, for instance regarding a mobile phone.

TODAY'S ISSUES FOR EMBEDDED LINUX

Although many consumer electronics products already use Embedded Linux, there are still many challenges to a widespread use of Embedded Linux in consumer electronics products.

Essential attributes that embedded systems need from their operating system are the following:

- Real-time capability.
- Fast boot-up time.
- Audio, video, and graphics functionality.
- Enhanced power management.
- Small system size and footprint.
- High degree of security.

REAL-TIME CAPABILITY

In communication devices, many components have always had the capability to function in real time, which means they always react within a given, often very short, time-frame. But this capability is also required for home entertainment devices. Take a DVD player for movies. Without real-time capability, frame losses, unnatural and patchy video play, or in the worst case, an interruption to play the video may occur. Those would be big usability problems.

With the advent of multi-processor architectures, one micro-processor, or Central Processing Unit (CPU), is used for real-time communications, and one CPU handles application processing. Here often a traditional real-time operating system is used for the communication CPU (such as the previously mentioned VxWorks or QNX) while Embedded Linux finds its place in the application CPU. Sometimes Embedded Linux has already been applied for the real-time part. However, it is still one of the main issues when looking for an expansion of Embedded Linux to a broader range of CE products. Therefore, to address a wide range of real-time requirements for consumer electronics devices, a dedicated working group in the CE Linux Forum is working to improve the real-time capabilities of Embedded Linux. As a result, the new CE Linux Forum specification released in June 2004 includes major improvements to the Linux kernel.[10]

This version of the specification has no specific comments on "hybrid" techniques that are already being used in the market, where, for instance, Embedded Linux runs on top of a small real-time operating system. Neither does it prevent the use of those hybrid techniques.

FAST BOOT-UP TIME

The time it takes to boot up is crucial in consumer electronics applications. Consumers are not used to waiting three minutes or so before a system is up and running after a power-on button is pressed, as they are in the PC world.

The issues here lie in the firmware (the whole software that resides in a device), the operating system kernel, and in the user space. The June 2004 specification of CE Linux defines features for

---

10. These improvements include an enhanced support for fixed priority preemptive scheduling and enhanced coverage of POSIX real-time API's support by Linux.

Embedded Linux that improve the boot-up time and includes other specifications supporting this.[11] For instance, non-existent devices will not be searched, or the system can be started directly from non-volatile memory.

AUDIO, VIDEO, AND GRAPHICS

Audio, video and graphics processing are essential functions for consumer electronics products, but no single (de facto) standard interfaces exits for this area. Having a well defined and well supported interface for audio, video, and graphics helps to reduce these fragmented solutions.

The aspects that are tackled to bring CE Linux further into its interaction capabilities are as follows:

- Establishing requirements for graphics and video presentation APIs from a kernel point of view.
- Identifying higher level APIs for video-input.
- Evaluating an Advanced Linux Sound Architecture.
- Defining frameworks for various audio, video, and graphics APIs.

POWER MANAGEMENT

For mobile devices or even for home electronics products like a digital TV, power management becomes a crucial aspect. For example, less heat is generated as lesser power is used. And the less power used, the longer the batteries last.

Typically, there are two approaches to power management.

- Designing and developing a low-power consumption circuit.
- Changing voltage or frequency dynamically according to the status of applications.

---

11. Calibration of delay avoidance, IDE no-probe option, and Kernel Execute-in-Place (XIP).

The first approach is sometimes called "static power management," while the second approach is called "dynamic power management." Basically with dynamic power management, voltage and frequency of a processor is reduced when an application goes idle.

In CE products, especially mobile phones or other handheld devices that are battery driven, efficient power management is critical to increase the battery life. Here power reduction methods such as voltage and frequency scaling, clock gating, power supply gating, input signal selection, and so on are used. The CE Linux Forum specification proposed the power management architecture considering the following two things:

- The design of a system-level optimization for power usage involving interactions among the application, the OS, and the hardware.

- The provision of a generic power management framework for various hardware platforms.

Also the platform specification classifies power management technologies into three categories: platform suspend/resume, device power management, and platform dynamic power management.

SYSTEM SIZE

The reduction of system size is not only a matter to save memory cost, but sometimes it has a tight relationship with boot-up time and real-time capabilities.

Embedded Linux is already in use by a wide-range of consumer electronics products. Some of them actually have enough resources to run quite large operating systems, but some of them do not. As cost competition in the consumer electronics market is extremely tough, even for those that have the capacity, the manufacturer will try to decrease memory consumption. So a balance of system size, implemented features, and performance is a key factor in the product design. The CE Linux Forum specification therefore defines a method to measure and compare the size between different Linux configurations, as well as techniques that may reduce the size. It also defines a set of standard mechanisms to reduce the system size and characterizes each method regarding its advantages and disadvantages.

SECURITY

When systems are networked and interoperating, security functions become crucial. When a device is attached to a network, it is exposed to various threats. The same is obviously true for an enterprise Linux. But as Embedded Linux sits in CE products, there is neither a system administrator nor specialist around who can change security parameters or update a virus protection system. Given this fact, it needs to be even more robust against security threats.

Key requirements are reliability, secure and trusted boot-up, access control, buffer and stack protection, intrusion detection, authentication, trusted connections such as SSL (Secure Socket Layer, used to securely exchange Web sites over the Internet), a firewall, secure field upgradeability, and so forth. Although only one technology (Protected RAM File System) is described in the CE Linux Forum specifications, many other technologies[12] to satisfy the requirements have been discussed and are described on the CE Linux Forum Web site.

FUTURE CHALLENGES: EMBEDDED LINUX

The two big Embedded Linux challenges for the near future are:

- Interoperability within an ecosystem.
- Quality management.

Embedded Linux vendors or CE manufacturers may modify Linux and develop their own versions of Linux. This imposes the threat of a fragmentation of Embedded Linux, which might lead to custom versions for many consumer electronics products.

---

12. Including Umbrella, LIDS (Linux Intrusion Defense System), Signed Binaries, TCG, etc.

This can best be overcome by creating a viable ecosystem where a number of different parties collaborate on developing a rich Embedded Linux while at the same time are competing in the marketplace.

Such an ecosystem is self-organized as consumer electronics manufacturers, device software vendors, software vendors, and service and content providers define and actively play their individual roles. (For more on roles in an ecosystem, see the "Keystone Concept" sidebar in Chapter 5, "Telehealthcare: The Key to the Living Room.")

We expect that this ecosystem will first evolve around service interfaces, which allow defined kinds of changes to a running system such as system patches, fixes, and extensions. The next step for Embedded Linux will therefore be a clear definition of service interfaces, including data formats and protocols.

QUALITY MANAGEMENT

Sometimes open source projects may incorporate untested and inconsistent fixes. It is already painful for PC users to apply patches that patch untested patches, but impossible in consumer electronics. The base system needs to be absolutely stable.

Staying at a proven code level (or version) is the easiest quality management ("never change a running system"), but sometimes you want to integrate the latest and greatest enhancements that have just been released by the open source communities. Currently, Linux distributors play in Enterprise Linux to provide these upgrades—and we expect the same to happen for Embedded Linux.

One option is also to create a test centre jointly run by CE manufacturers and Linux distributors to ensure a certain version of Embedded Linux meets their quality requirements. A mechanism to automatically apply critical fixes to consumer electronics products without any user intervention would be used to distribute these quality assured versions.

CONCLUSION

Where are embedded systems going? They are going further and faster than we're ready to think about. Embedded systems are commonplace today, but in few years they will be more than commonplace. They will be everywhere.

In the future, the market for embedded information processing will grow to dwarf that for desktop and server machines. And Embedded Linux looks to be the best bet for a de facto standard for the operating system that will control the lion's share of those embedded systems.

10

Software Development Strategies for Connected Consumer Electronics

Paul Brody

In the future, consumer electronics devices will no longer be stand-alone. Instead, they will be highly connected components that interact with each other. This vision of convergence and connectivity has been a long time coming and has now arrived. Today, connectivity is primarily done via PCs and hard-wired connections (such as synchronization of PDAs and music players), but in the future, individual CE devices will be themselves directly connected to the Internet as well to each other. And it is software that is making most of it happen.

While standards for most features may gradually emerge, successful first movers will be the companies that blaze a trail, enabling seamless connectivity across devices and networks. However, the challenge is not to simply enable connectivity, but to make the user experience seamless, simple, and intuitive. Complex fussy software that requires configuration or does not "just work" will be a path to failure.

Software quality and capability will be one of the key determinants of success in the future state electronics industry. Companies that can create simple, effective, and integrated systems will be positioned for success. Those that depend entirely on licensed and standardized solutions will find themselves mere commodity merchants living on forever plunging margins.

Software has been a part of consumer electronics since the industry's beginning. From portable CD players to toasters, embedded software has always had a role to play. In the future, that role will grow from minor to dominant. Already most consumer electronics companies employ more software developers than hardware engineers. Going forward, software must do much more than find the optimal toasting time for a frozen bagel or, as IBM's managing director for Philips, Piet Bill, touts it, "Experience is becoming more important than the device providing it, and those companies that provide the best holistic ambient experience will be the leaders of that new era."

THE BLOCKBUSTER PRODUCTS OF 2010 ARE ALREADY HERE

The consumer electronics industry's mega products in 2010 may already be here. The original iPod was introduced in 2001. The first hand-held MP3 player was the Diamond Multimedia Rio 300, introduced in 1998. The Blackberry's predecessor, the RIM Interactive Pager, arrived in 1996.[1] None of today's blockbuster products were recognized as such the day they were introduced— their concepts were too alien to the business and consumer environments at the time. These products were continuously improved and, through word of mouth and demonstrated ease of use, emerged as leaders. What might seem like a sudden arrival is usually anything but.

Though most consumers continue to think of consumer electronics as physical items, many of the most innovative and successful

---

1. From *MobilePC* magazine's list of the top 100 gadgets of all time, at www.mobilepcmag.com/features/2005_03/top100gadgets.html.

products depend on software and content for their differentiation. While it is impossible to predict what will be driving the consumer electronics market in 2010, we can see products today that are, to a greater or lesser degree, consistent with our vision of consumer electronics as networked systems driven by software and content. These products are discussed in the following sections.

HONDA'S XM NAVTRAFFIC ON ACURA CARS

The newest Acura cars contain an integrated satellite navigation system with a difference—real-time traffic updates. Location is provided by the GPS system, maps are read from a car-level DVD player, and traffic information is delivered in real time via XM Satellite Radio data streaming. With this integrated system, drivers don't simply get to their destination; they get around traffic bottlenecks along the way.

MOTOROLA IRADIO

Motorola's iRadio product integrates the ability to play personal music libraries like an iPod with a selection of commercial-free radio channels into a mobile telephone. Equipped for personal headphones or car stereo integration, the iRadio product will efficiently leverage home broadband connections for downloading pre-recorded radio and live wireless connections for up-to-the-minute content such as news and talk-radio. iRadio will be the first consumer product that delivers Motorola's vision of seamless mobility, allowing users to take their personal music from the home PC into their cars and everywhere else they go.[2]

APPLE IPOD + ITUNES

Overexposed and over-hyped as it may be, the iPod, in combination with iTunes, remains one of the effective examples of how

---

2. The Engadget Interview: Dave Ulmer, Motorola Media Solutions. Posted April 4, 2005, www.engadget.com.

software can transform a product. Alone, the iPod is a stylish MP3 player, but when paired with iTunes and the online store, the iPod provides an impressive demonstration of how seamless integration can hide the complexity of digital rights management and synchronization across devices and networks.

KODAK EASYSHARE ONE CAMERA

This digital camera when combined with the WiFi accessory allows users to take and share pictures with the touch of a button. The whole solution will integrate the device with Kodak's printing and online photo services enabling pictures to be shared with friends and family.

CHALLENGES IN DEVELOPMENT

Products like the ones just described share some common characteristics that make them much more complex and challenging to develop and deliver than traditional CE products. These are the very traits that we expect to be standard on all consumer electronics products over the next five years: secure content, systems integration, and seamless mobility.

The need for secure content delivery management, whether private content such as email and photos or published content such as music or video, is critical for consumers. The most distinctive products are likely to be those that are able to seamlessly mix and integrate multiple streams of content and weave together private content with published content.

Examples of mixing content streams are already emerging. The iPod photo seems to show that consumers want to set their pictures to music. The Honda XM-based navigation system mixes public information from GPS sources and weather systems with private data on traffic status to create new value for drivers. These integrations present opportunities to add value to information steams that are individually available free of charge, such as US weather data.[3]

With the end of stand-alone consumer electronics, systems integration is another key characteristic of future consumer electronics. Convergence has often been thought of as the ability for consumer electronics to perform multiple functions, but this is a vision that has never come true. Instead, consumers have consistently chosen products for their superior usability rather than their breadth of functionality. However, these "deep function" products are increasingly integrated systems that incorporate a client device and software along with server-side systems and network connectivity.

Network connectivity and more specifically, seamless mobility, is the other key characteristic of future consumer electronics. Pradma Sree Warrior, Motorola's CTO, defines seamless connectivity as the ability to move content, voice conversations, and other interactions across networks and devices without interruption. Anson Chen, Motorola's chief of software development, compares software enabling mobility to the advent of the Web browser in importance.

Connectivity is the ingredient that ties together the other elements of future consumer electronics—integrated systems and secure content streams. Connectivity permits content to be moved and constantly updated, as well as protected through validation and authorization where necessary. Connectivity also permits live interaction and the delivery of new services and information on demand. While devices such as the iPod work effectively in offline mode, consumers regard connecting to a PC to get new music as a necessary hassle, not a benefit.

Essentially all these capabilities are enabled by software development skills. Without iTunes, the iPod is a very attractive and well

---

3. Boyle, James, "Public Information Wants to Be Free," *Financial Times Online,* February 24, 2005.

designed MP3 player but probably not positioned for market dominance. Without the distinctive TiVo[4] software, with its famous ability to guess the most personal preferences of its owners based on their viewing habits, a TiVo box is just another hard drive with a video capture card.[5]

NEW SKILLS FOR A NEW ERA

Traditional software development for consumer electronics has been fairly simple. For example, defrosting and toasting a bagel requires specific data inputs and outputs and can be managed by a very reliable algorithm. To be successful, the world of networked consumer electronics requires an altogether different set of software development capabilities.

We believe that there are five critical skills that the consumer electronics industry must master in the area of software development to be successful in the future. These skills are systems engineering, architecture management, collaborative management, content protection, and iterative development and configuration management. The fact that none of these skills relate to actually writing/debugging lines of code may explain why new entrants have had such a disruptive effect on the CE market recently and why traditional consumer electronics companies have been so slow to respond effectively.

SYSTEMS ENGINEERING

The top-priority skill to obtain is systems engineering. This is a discipline more familiar to aviation companies and defense contractors than to consumer electronics businesses. Systems engineering is the discipline of designing complex systems that reliably

---

4. TiVo Inc. sells a personal video recorder to capture television programs on an internal hard disk and allows a time-shifted playback with the option to remove advertisements.
5. Zaslow, Jeffrey, "Oh no! My TiVo thinks I'm gay," *The Wall Street Journal*, December 2002.

function across platforms, across networks, and around the world in a seamless and reliable manner.

The work of systems engineering is to map out all the systems and users involved in the solution and their interactions together. Defense contractors have long had a proper understanding of systems engineering. Network warfare technologies must integrate information from agents in the field, satellite reconnaissance, and databases into a single, actionable data stream usable by soldiers in the field. Data must flow securely but in near real time, around the world and across networks of varying quality and reliability.

Similarly, the design of connected and integrated consumer products will require significant skills. Very soon, we will take it for granted that a song purchased online can be delivered to our mobile phones, our cars, and our home PCs, but the services that support this process are indeed very complex.

Between selecting, paying, delivering, and listening to the desired content, a dozen systems must interact, such as mobile networks, phone companies, record companies, and banks. While the individual connections between systems may seem trivial, when millions of credit card transactions are processed online every day, the number of connections increases the complexity of the system.

ARCHITECTURE MANAGEMENT

Architecture management is another critical skill that CE companies must embrace to become successful in the future. A well-managed architecture is the key that will enable consumer electronics companies to turn products into platforms and to turn market leadership into profitable growth.

Product architecture governs how individual aspects of a product work together to form a robust, functioning whole. In well-architected systems, requirements are associated with individual functional elements, and each element of the architecture has a defined interaction with other elements. As a result, the elements of the architecture are modular and re-usable.

The payoff from architecture management arrives when markets mature and grow around an individual product. Companies can saturate the market with variations on the original product at very little cost. They also can disassociate the core software from the original hardware and begin licensing the functionality and code, leveraging the speed and energy of Original Design Manufacturers (ODMs) and electronics companies targeting the Opening Price Point at major retailers like Wal-Mart.

So significant is the leverage from architecture management that at Motorola, the company is organizing two cross-enterprise centers of excellence around this capability. The first, a Standards & Architecture group, will work to define standards and architectures that will be adhered to across the group, enabling connectivity and reuse across the company's wide range of infrastructure and consumer products from hand-held radios to mobile phones to mobile network base stations. The second group, Common Platforms, is taking those standards and driving them into reusable platforms that can support a diverse range of specific products.

Architecting products to work seamlessly across platforms and networks is very difficult. In immature markets with rapidly changing technology, the ability to control the entire product including hardware, software, and network environment in a closed loop system is a key competitive advantage. The success of Apple and RIM in their respective markets has come from their tight control and focus on quality. It's no accident that MP3 players other than the iPod are often panned by reviewers for their complexity and poor usability.

As markets mature, however, the playing field can change dramatically, and well architected systems can close the usability gap. The architecture-centric approach is the core of Microsoft's efforts to come from behind and take dominant positions in the mobile media and messaging businesses. Though not yet successful, Microsoft is harnessing the legions of nimble ODMs to create new products and flood the market.

To varying degrees, both Apple and RIM have responded to this challenge by opening their systems and licensing technology and solutions to other players like Motorola. However, executives at CE companies say that Microsoft's ability to build easy-to-implement platforms is virtually unequalled. Cyberhome Entertainment, one of the newest and fastest-growing consumer electronics companies, has already chosen to go with a Microsoft platform for mobile media products. Microsoft's well-architected products mean that the cost of bringing new solutions to market compares favourably with just about any other option, including open source.

WHITHER OPEN SOURCE?

Open source software is much more than free software; it is a movement by consumers and businesses to take back control of the software on which they depend. For consumers, open source software offers much of the same appeal that enterprises see in it: It's not only free, but it frees them from the risk that a key supplier will be able to change the terms and conditions associated with the product after they've already committed to using it.

By its very nature, open source software does away with many of the problems that anger consumers with commercial solutions. Because the software tends to be developed by public committees, over-reaching the business model is not possible. The collaborative nature of the development process also tends to result in much better documentation of requirements, better structured architecture, and ultimately, much better quality software.

Open source should be positioned well to dominate consumer electronics, but in fact it suffers from several drawbacks that may well prevent it from having a leading role in the space. The open source software movement tends to be philosophically hostile to the digital rights management aspirations of the major content providers. Open source programmers are more likely to be famous for cracking DRM schemes than building them, but without content protection, open source solutions will never gain legal access to content.

continues

One other key obstacle for open source solutions is that they tend not to be as simple to use and implement as packaged applications from providers like Microsoft. Open source solutions are created by and tend to appeal to more sophisticated software developers, but it is the legion of contract manufacturers and ODMs across Asia that are critical to win over. For the most part, these companies have few software development assets in-house. "Packaged solutions from Microsoft give us branding and time to market we can't get anywhere else," says Cyberhome's Wu.

Companies like RedHat have already proven that successful stand-alone business models can be developed around open source software. And companies like TiVo have demonstrated that you can build robust, secure content protection into Linux-based devices, but the examples are relatively few and far between. To achieve the same power in consumer electronics as corporate servers, open source developers will need to focus on bundling easy-to-mplement solutions in the consumer space and engage with standards bodies around content protection issues.

COLLABORATIVE DEVELOPMENT

No one company will control the future state environment from end to end. Consumer electronics systems must interact across networks, with content providers, retailers, and service providers, not to mention home networks and users. Enabling seamless mobility and connectivity will require a high degree of collaboration across many enterprises.

Consider the requirements to enable mobile phone users to switch from a wireless voice-over IP (VOIP) system in the office to a public mobile network on the drive home and then on to their home VOIP system when they arrive. The call must pass seamlessly across a corporate IT network, a public mobile network, and then into a home network environment, each with hardware and software controlled by different organizations.

Enabling such a complex interaction requires significant collaboration. For Motorola, it has meant building close collaborative ties with companies like Cisco and Avaya, as well as their traditional partners, cellular network operators.

"While standardized APIs and SDKs will emerge in the long run to enable ease of interoperation, those are characteristics of mature environments. If you want to be first to market, you must make collaboration a strategic priority," says Motorola's Chen.

The discipline of collaborative development encompasses the set of skills required to deliver these complex interactive products. The ability to clearly define requirements, share requirements, gather back the results, and test them in an efficient manner—and to do all this across enterprise boundaries is the essence of collaborative development. This skill set is crucial, not just for bringing products to market with the collaboration of other key players, but also for developing software in a global environment—handing off development to partners around the world 24 hours a day.

Successful collaborative development requires not only a business structured around collaboration, but also the process discipline and infrastructure to execute. Collaborative development is a highly disciplined process—demanding clear documentation of requirements, inputs, and outputs. Companies that know how to do systems engineering and develop system architectures are usually well prepared to do collaborative product development. Infrastructure is also required not only to manage the volume of activity around the clock, but also to drive process discipline. Well-designed systems prompt partners and developers to follow the best practice processes and adhere to good design standards.

CONTENT PROTECTION

Access and ability to distribute and use content is permitted at the discretion of the copyright holder. Today, it is impossible to think of consumer electronics that are not increasingly dependent on access to content of one kind or another. Even the refrigerator and microwave are likely to become access devices for content on cooking and recipes as they become networked appliances.

There are good arguments for making much more content free of charge. Recent studies show that, for example, the "free" data streams from the US Government on weather conditions and GPS data are creating whole new industries. Nonetheless, the bulk of commercial content is likely to remain under strict private control. Consumer electronics companies that want branded content in their distribution networks will need to demonstrate they can protect that content from widespread copying.

Robust content protection stands on three key capabilities. First and foremost, a hardware-based "root of trust" is essential. Hardware-based systems significantly raise the bar for reverse engineering and decryption compared to software-only systems. Secondly, advanced content protection systems must be remotely renewable with updated schemes as content-protection strategies are hacked and must be revised. Lastly, a set of forensic capabilities is required to identify the device responsible for distributing content into the public domain. That device can then be disabled. No content protection system will be 100 percent certain, but systems with these capabilities are less likely to be widely broken.[6]

In winning over consumers, the key challenge in content protection is to be un-intrusive. Existing Digital Rights Management (DRM) systems are widely disliked for their ability to make individual users feel like criminals and prevent them from doing things they have long taken for granted—such as moving content between their personal devices. In this respect, increased use of Broadcast Flags that tie the ability to use content to a device or network of devices rather than an individual user may be much less intrusive.

Content protection remains an especially immature capability in the CE industry. While there are a number of industry consortia that are working to establish standards, many of these standards, such as the "Advanced Access Content System" (AACS) and the HD Broadcast Flag system, are becoming established; these individual systems tend to cover a specific media or format. As the standards become established and mature, it will be possible to

---

6.   Interview with Tom Bellwood & Kelvin Lawrence, IBM.

simply license a control mechanism, but until then, there is significant value to be added by electronics companies that know how to make the implementation of a standard seamless and transparent to end users.

ITERATIVE DEVELOPMENT & CONFIGURATION MANAGEMENT

In the 1970s and 1980s, companies like Sony lead the industry not only with great design and quality, but with a commitment to continuous improvement. Portable radios and Walkmans just kept getting smaller and sleeker, going forever on one battery. The same is true in software, where continuous improvement is required and indeed expected.

As consumer electronics products become dependent on complex software developed collaboratively across multiple enterprises, the importance of following a rigorous development methodology grows. The more complex the software, the more likely it is to be developed behind schedule and full of bugs. Additionally, as consumer electronics companies attempt to proliferate their software across multiple platforms (think iTunes in your car, on your phone, on your iPod, on your home PC), the complexity of managing compatibility across those devices becomes a tremendous burden.

To meet this challenge, developers need to alter their approach to creating and managing software. The lone coder working late into the night on Coke and pizza is being replaced by global teams that hand off development across time zones. The most advanced development methodology available is based on a risk-adjusted rapid iteration strategy. Known commonly as "Iterative Development," it has several branded variations, including the "Rational Unified Process" offered by IBM.[7]

Common to all the variations is an approach that is very focused on rigorous system architecture and rapid design-test-delivery cycles. In the world of iterative development, products are

---

7.　Rational Unified Process and the Rational Unified Process for Systems Engineering are methodologies offered by IBM's Rational Software division.

decomposed into their most basic functions. The ones considered the most important and the riskiest are done first in a complete cycle of design, development, test, and delivery. Subsequent iterations add features while testing runs continuously. Companies that comply with the best practices of iterative development deliver their software in half the time and with far fewer problems than comparable solutions delivered the traditional way.[8]

Once software is ready and operating across multiple platforms, consumer electronics companies must learn how to manage that software and control for compatibility issues. For example, a new BMW 5 or 7 Series sedan will have more than 25 computer modules onboard and hundreds of separate programs running. Automakers receive updates to system software running on these processors, on average, once a week, for bug fixes and performance improvements. At any given time, thousands, if not millions, of different software-version combinations could exist on the cars being produced and already in service.[9]

This complexity is a problem because, while new software updates are designed to work with all previous versions of companion software, in practice that is often not true. The more devices that interact with each other, the greater the probability that users will experience odd or unpredictable system behaviour. Because it is impossible to test every combination of software, manufacturers must maintain selected lists of known valid configurations.

Companies with strong configuration management skills will be better able to manage the quality of their products and assure interoperability as they push common software across their own products and license it out to other enterprises. New technologies, such as RFID, will make it easier to maintain configuration. RFID tags carry enough information not just to identify the product being produced and sold as a category, but to identify the specific product being purchased, including its configuration at the time of

---

8. IBM Internal and Customer Experiences. Improvements are representative of typical gains, but some companies have reported significantly better gains in specific cases.
9. IBM Customer Experiences.

production and purchase. Network connectivity will also permit that configuration information to be remotely tracked and managed as it changes over time.[10]

TAKING THE RIGHT ACTIONS

Like all engineering activities, software development is an essentially creative activity. The most talented development organizations consistently produce software that is leaps and bounds superior to competitors. Elegant and easy to use, consumers need never open the manual. In the future, the creative and elegant solutions that make software simple must extend far beyond the user interface.

Investments made by consumer electronics companies to build up software developments skills are essentially about upgrading skills and concentrating that creativity on the highest return activities. For a creative and intellectually challenging job, software developers today still spend far too much of their time re-inventing the wheel. Capabilities like iterative development, architecture management, and configuration management allow development organizations to focus on their highest value-add work, not on rewriting code to cross platforms or re-inventing functions that have already been developed and work well.

The transformation from a hardware-focused CE company to a complex systems integrator can take time. Transformation cannot be accomplished overnight, and no single company can build the full set of skills required for success in consumer electronics. Consequently, companies with winning strategies are the ones that are focused and selective; like their products, they are deep in their chosen areas of expertise and ruthless in outsourcing those that don't fit.

The right choice of skills to build will vary depending on the segment of the consumer electronics industry. While everything may well end up being networked, consumers are unlikely to take their

---

10. IBM RFID & Wireless Emerging Business Opportunity groups; IBM Research.

refrigerators around with them, so skills in mobility may not be important in white goods. No matter what your focus, though, there are specific actions that every consumer electronics company should take. These are discussed in the following four sections.

CREATE AND IMPLEMENT A SOFTWARE STRATEGY

Software development has often been an afterthought at CE companies. As a result, software organizations are often anything but organized: distributed across the company, embedded in hardware development teams, or contracted out to third parties. While electronics have achieved six sigma quality levels in hardware, the same level of maturity has not been developed for software.

Basic blocking and tackling can go a long way to improving performance and results. It is critical to establish common systems and metrics for all software developers and to build centers of competency. Furthermore, companies should centralize their software development functions and build an internal market for those services. Done right, this can lead to a dramatic improvement in skills and competency around best-practice methodologies.

Common tools and methodology across an enterprise are also critical. Without these, it is impossible for software developers to move easily from one project to another or to hand off work between time zones. Establishing common tools can also have a dramatic effect on the cost of managing the IT environment in software development, freeing up money for real engineering work.[11]

The most advanced engineering companies are already oriented toward software development. Over 75 percent of Motorola's engineers are now focused on software development, and Motorola's CTO, Padmasree Warrior, sees licensing and technology transfer, particularly in the software field, as key to driving Motorola's vision of seamless mobility into a global standard.

---

11. "Improving Innovation and Cash Flow in High Tech Manufacturing," AMR Research, August 19, 2003.

START AT THE TOP OF THE PROCESS

Whatever the long-term software development strategy, in-sourced or out-sourced, proprietary or open, transformation begins at the "top" of the process with requirements definition. Companies that cannot document their requirements will never be able to prioritize, outsource, or collaborate on development, nor will they be able to properly test the product once it is built.

A negative cycle of poor requirements management is easy to start: Late-arriving requirements are often a key source of problems in product delays, cost over-runs, and quality. Incomplete requirements that go to vendors who seek changes and clarifications continuously add to the confusion. As the requirements change, those changes are never documented, so not only is it difficult to test the product once completed, but the requirements are not in one place so that they could be easily found for re-use.

DEVELOP A CONTENT DISTRIBUTION STRATEGY

Intellectual property assets are critical gating items. If you can't license a piece of software or content, your product may end up, relative to other solutions, crippled. Branded content, in particular, offers few substitutes. There is only one Eric Clapton, and an online music catalog without him or the Beatles is likely to be at a distinct competitive disadvantage.

Consumer electronics companies are not entirely at the mercy of content providers, however. Most content businesses are hit-driven, and the bulk of profits come from a few blockbuster artists, movies, and television shows. The bulk of content is unprofitable today, but it does not always have to be that way. In a world of physical distribution, keeping inventory of all the CDs made every year is impossibly expensive, and much content that might have only niche appeal is simply not available. In a digital environment, every piece of content can be kept alive. Consumer electronics companies can offer a vast new sales channel.

"If you want a single blockbuster movie, the studio will dictate the terms and you can just roll over and play dead," says Derek

Alderton, a consultant experienced in music and video licensing business. "If you have a way to improve the profitability of an entire catalog, the content providers will sit up and listen to you."

SECURE CONNECTIVITY FOR YOUR PRODUCTS

In the future, seamless connectivity will be as important for consumer electronics products as content delivery. Personal interactions, from email to instant messaging, already drive profitability in mobile devices. Multi-player games will depend on connectivity if they are to go mobile, and content protection schemes may require periodic connectivity to re-authorize access.

As the cost of chipsets for mobile telephony, GSM or EV-DO,[12] declines, more and more electronics will come with those capabilities standard. However, outside the home, wireless connectivity is usually neither free nor easy to establish. Consumers are unlikely to pay monthly subscription fees for many different services or devices. This sets up a conflict between multi-purpose devices that include mobile service and stand-alone devices that may offer superior functionality.

Consumer electronics companies will need to develop alternative business models based on per-use or one-time fees that include connectivity. Already video game companies are including online service as part of the purchase price rather than as a monthly subscription in some cases.

AVOIDING THE WRONG ACTIONS

There are also business practices that companies would be smart to avoid as they go forward. One of the biggest challenges in products that are defined by their software is the enormous flexibility and capability that software offers. Hardware systems imposed a

---

12. GSM—*Global System for Mobile Communications* and EV-DO—*Evolution Data Only* are mobile phone standards, with the latter being an upgrade to the CDMA (*Code Division Multiple Access*) standard that is widely used in North America, Japan, Korea, and Israel.

discipline on developers that kept them from putting too many buttons on radios or too many different functions. With software, some of that creativity must be controlled in the interest of making products easy to use and own. Some of the most obvious mistakes that are already emerging are discussed here.

OVERREACHING THE BUSINESS MODEL

Business models come in and out of fashion. At the moment, the most popular is some variation of the "razor and blades" or the "annuity" model. The assumption is that, once "hooked," customers will keep coming back for more. Embedded software in products has allowed companies to extend this concept as never before.

While it is hard to precisely draw the line between optimizing the business model and overreaching, there are certain clear signs of over-reach that are likely to provoke the fury of consumers. First and foremost are software updates that change or restrict product functionality after it has already been purchased.

Recent examples of consumer electronics companies walking between optimization and over-reach—or crossing it—include Apple and TiVo. For all its finesse, Apple is risking a customer backlash with recent restrictions on CD burning and streaming that came, unannounced, in new version of iTunes. TiVo launched pop-up ads that appear when consumers fast-forward through broadcast commercials, another "feature" that is generating heated discussion among user groups online.

CE companies will be well advised to appoint consumer and privacy advocates to vet software-driven changes and create a software model that makes these upgrades optional to customers, particularly in less-mature software categories where published and open standards do not prevail yet. As standards emerge, for example in the area of content protection, large committees of Hollywood Studios, electronics companies, and regulators make sudden changes difficult to achieve. By contrast, in closed loop proprietary systems such as iTunes+iPod or TiVo, changes to functionality are dangerously easy to implement.

CONFUSING CONSUMERS WITH ENTERPRISES

Consumer electronics is, as the name suggests, about consumers: individuals and families, not large enterprises. In some ways, the gap between consumers and businesses is starting to close. All of a sudden, consumers do indeed find themselves managing networks, worrying about security, interoperability, and even Total Cost of Ownership (TCO). However, the analogy should not be taken too far.

Overall, consumers are much freer to experiment with new systems and technologies. They are less concerned about ten-year TCO or deployment and training costs and more interested in functionality. While this is not a pass to develop inflexible solutions based on totally proprietary solutions, it does mean that functionality and completeness of experience should trump open architecture and standards compliance for less-mature areas.

In the long run, as markets mature, products should indeed converge with standards as they become established. Case in point: instant messaging. This service originated as a consumer product but has gradually penetrated the enterprise. Similarly, mobile devices will penetrate the enterprise market from the consumer side as well. The Blackberry has been a hit product, and RIM celebrated the two millionth active user after five years in the market, just like the Sony PlayStation Portable has already sold three million units in its first four months on the market.[13]

Perhaps the biggest difference between consumers and enterprises is likely to be around business models and content protection and management. Consumers do not license software or content; in their minds, they are buying a product. The click-through license that most consumers hit "Yes" to in about one second when installing the P2P program Kazaa on their PCs runs to 22,606 words on 182 on-screen pages and even then it refers to license

---

13. "Sony May Outsource Production of PlayStation Portable (Update1)," *Bloomberg*, May 26, 2005

agreements that are not shown in that screen.[14] None of that verbiage will protect consumer electronics companies from the fury of consumers who feel they have been treated unfairly.

CONCLUSION

It would be silly to predict the exact blockbuster consumer products of 2010 today, though some of them might be sitting at the back of a store somewhere or taking up a small portion of current shelf space. Still, just like a savvy individual investor, companies can place intelligent bets on key skills and capabilities that will leave them well positioned. A good return will come from being ready for a future in which consumer electronics are highly connected, converged, and integrated devices used by sophisticated and mobile consumers.

Software skills will separate the consumer electronics companies that create value from those that are confined in the commodity hardware space of the market, licensing all their solutions. Companies that choose to go the path of pure in-licensing will surely find themselves consistently last to market. That said, no electronics company can afford to build the complete spectrum of skills required internally. Instead, focus, timing, and readiness to embrace change will be critical. As capabilities move from the bleeding edge to common-place, the skills associated with those capabilities become commodities as well, and licensing more becomes attractive.

Lastly, consumer electronics companies ignore the skills and creativity of their customers at their peril. From Google to Windows Mobile to Palm Pilots to Linux, platforms that leverage the creativity and skills of the customer base are sure to thrive. From online user forums to home-developed software and "hacks," consumer electronics customers are more firmly in control of the product direction than ever before.

---

14. Edelman, Ben, "Comparison of Unwanted Software Installed by P2P Programs," available at www.benedelman.org.

11

Differentiation Through Product and User Interface Design

Paul Brody, Hagen Wenzek, Tom Osterday

Technological convergence between consumer electronics, mobile telephony, and personal computers has resulted in a dramatic increase in the intensity and variety of competitive products in the CE industry. Common components and highly-efficient procurement business practices enable companies like Dell and HP to enter traditional consumer electronics markets that used to be dominated by companies such as Sony and Matsushita with an immediately competitive offering.

Though it is still possible to be technologically distinctive, the combined raise of sophisticated Original Design Manufacturers (ODMs) and software licensors for consumer electronics (like Microsoft) are reducing the market window for capturing a price premium from technology alone. When a new capability is developed, work-alike devices are faster to market. Sophisticated buying organizations, such as Wal-Mart, are also quick to spot and develop suppliers who can supply advanced technology products at their "Opening Price Point," the lowest price solution.

VICIOUS COMMODITIZATION

The result of this technological convergence and component standardization is a market full of undifferentiated look-alike and work-alike products. From LCD televisions to portable DVD players to MP3 players, competition tends to become centered on specifications, such as size and weight, and most importantly, price. Competition in these commoditized markets is fierce, and companies that are on the top of the market one year can find themselves quickly removed by a competitor or new upstart with better supply of key components the next year.

In addition to locking companies into long-term low-margin businesses, this cycle of standardization and continuous competition is imposing an enormous cost of complexity on the CE industry. Far from being simple, managing commodity supply chains is enormously challenging, complex, and expensive. As befits true commodities, demand for undifferentiated consumer electronics is enormously volatile. Slight changes in price and features can send demand for one brand of LCD TV soaring and the other plunging. This volatility whiplashes back through the entire supply chain, leading to surges and plunges of demand for components depending on who is winning the price and market share battle this week. The "winners" pay ludicrous premiums to buy components on the open market, and the "losers" write off large purchase commitments or inventories.

Commoditized products also result in ludicrously short life cycles and new product introductions that do not represent meaningful improvements that consumers really care about. The differences across product generations are increasingly small, but the cost of complexity for managing new part numbers, product obsolescence, and phase in/out planning is very high. Furthermore, with generous return privileges, consumers feel quite comfortable returning products that are the least bit difficult to use or that they saw advertised elsewhere for less. Return rates for new consumer electronics can often run up to 30 percent, a crippling financial and operational burden.

This cycle of continuous commoditization and needless operational complexity is not predestined for consumer electronics companies. There are ways to grow market share without introducing new products every six weeks. There are ways to increase prices for new products and to avoid the trap of volatile commodity demand—it is through creating products with distinctive and superior design and user interfaces and products that are intuitive to use and stylish to be seen using. Done well, these products are not just profitable; they can also revitalize entire companies and brands.

APPLE & SAMSUNG: A TALE OF TWO COMEBACKS

When you talk about consumer electronics, you will talk about two companies that are striking examples for transformation. We "had to" mention them throughout this book, too. Let us explore what their story is from a brand perspective.

SAMSUNG'S LEAPFROGGING

Just before the turn of the century, Korea's Samsung Electronics Company was the industry's lowest common denominator. Samsung's products were considered low-end and were sold in Kmart, Wal-Mart, and similar discount stores. As such, Samsung's products had just one major advantage over its competitors: a cheaper price. But price alone doesn't win consumers' hearts. Recognizing this, Samsung decided to focus on product design. Today, Samsung is moving uptown. Samsung's brand value has more than doubled since 2000, from $5.22 billion to $10.85 billion. In just two years, from 2001 to 2003, Samsung leapfrogged from the number 42 spot[1] on the list of the world's most valuable

---

1. "Scoreboard: The 100 Top Brands," *BusinessWeek Online,* August 6, 2001, www.businessweek.com/magazine/content/01_32/b3744010.htm.

brands to spot number 25 and continues to climb (2005: 20).[2] No other company's climb comes close.[3]

While increases in brand value can be driven by increased advertising spending, low prices, or high quality, Samsung took another route and made product design the centrepiece of its transformation. The results are that in just five years, Samsung's product designs have garnered 18 prestigious Industrial Design Excellence Awards (IDEAs) from the Industrial Designers Society of America—a record that is second only to Apple's.

APPLE'S COMEBACK

Apple's own turnaround story started at the brink of bankruptcy. Apple's key to competitive success is cool design. From the candy-coloured iMacs of 1998 to the sleek, white iBooks of today, cutting-edge design has done much to restore Apple's shine. Today, the Apple brand is considered the 41st most valuable in the world, despite spending far less than more highly ranked players. While Apple's turn-around has had a lot to do with managing some challenging software transitions well, it's surging brand value is very much driven by the cool factor in their products and is much less attributed to excessive marketing spend.

Apple's market-leading MP3 player, the iPod, delivers basically the same functions as its competitors' products but commands a price premium of as much as 50 percent due to a sleek, clean design that is both practical and beautiful. Apple is estimated to have captured between 60 and 90 percent of the global market for MP3 players. The iPod is a prime example of the premium commanded by superior design. In the past, when consumer electronics were much more expensive, buying decisions were driven by price advantages and feature differences. Today, as consumer electronics become less expensive and less differentiated, buying decisions are driven more and more by product design.

---

2. "The Global Brand Scoreboard—The 100 Top Brands," *BusinessWeek*, August 1, 2005.
3. "When the Butterfly Flaps Its Wings." IBM Institute for Business Value Executive Brief, 2003.

The payoff to Apple from superior branding and design has come not just from increased revenues. The company has also been able to moderate the pace of new product introductions and price reductions, especially with the iPod. While others have been routinely slashing prices and introducing slightly modified MP3 players without any impact, Apple's new product introductions tend to occur infrequently and generate excitement as they often represent step-change improvements to the products, such as doubling battery life or adding picture capability to high-end models. And while other CE companies know that a back-ordered product is a lost sale, Apple's customers will often wait weeks for delivery of their stylish products.

FINDING THE DESIGN FORMULA

The growing link between innovative style and strong brand value is evident. Other electronics companies that have benefited from the advantages of superior product design include IBM with 17 IDEA Awards, Hewlett-Packard with 14 awards, and Microsoft with 11 awards.[4] In spite of this trend, electronics companies that focus on style remain in the minority.

Although winning designs occasionally are achieved using current industry processes, producing such designs on a consistent basis requires focus, discipline, and a radically different approach to product development. Tom Kelly, General Manager of the prominent design firm IDEO, touts an approach to this challenge that integrates the concepts of classical corporate R&D departments and innovative designers.[5]

RAMP-UP DESIGN TEAMS

Samsung is one company that is following this approach. The company has changed its development approach by doubling its design staff to 350 in the past five years and changing its reporting structure to give stylists greater authority. Designers once reported to

4.   IBM Business Consulting Services analysis, 2004.
5.   Kelly, Tom. *The Art of Innovation,* Doubleday: New York, NY, 2001.

engineers and product planners, but now command equal levels of authority in the company. Collaboration with the rest of the company is considered key. Design teams work across the company, collaborating with everyone from blue-sky market researchers and manufacturing experts to engineers, thereby tapping the company's full breadth of expertise.[6]

NEW PRODUCT DEVELOPMENT MODELS

Other leading companies, too, have changed their product development models. In setting out to revitalize Apple, CEO Steve Jobs purposely implemented a new product development model, teaming Jon Rubinstein, a practical electrical engineer, with Jonathan Ive. Together, the team has led the development of such Apple hits as the titanium PowerBook G4 laptop and the sleek iBook laptops. The two men complement and balance one another, with the engineer vetoing the stylist's more outrageous design ideas and the stylist pushing to make every new product a design innovation.[7]

"CHIEF DESIGN EXECUTIVE"

At Sony, a different approach can be seen. Lead stylist Teiyu Goto and his team operate with unprecedented autonomy and authority, answering only to top management. The design team wages ongoing battles with Sony's engineers so that good design consistently trumps issues of engineering difficulty. The belief driving this changed product development model is "if we don't constantly create something new and grow the business, Sony is finished."[8] Superior styling has long been credited with keeping Sony consumer electronics at premium price points even as rivals strive to close the technology gap.

---

6. "Pink-Haired Designers, Red Cell Phones—Ka-Ching!" *BusinessWeek Online,* June 16, 2003.
7. Tam, Pui-Wing. "Designing Team Helps Shape Apple Computer's Fortunes." *The Wall Street Journal,* July 18, 2001.
8. Guth, Robert A. "Details, Details." *The Wall Street Journal*, October 1, 2001.

ADVANCED MECHANICAL DESIGN TOOLS

Whirlpool is using advanced mechanical design tools in its product development model to capture market share. The company is cost-effectively creating market-specific variations of its products based on consumer preferences in different countries. For example, Whirlpool developed different versions of its new, low-cost washing machine, which features four long legs for consumers in Brazil, casters for consumers in India, and a foldable top for consumers in China, based on the company's market research concerning consumer preferences. Whirlpool produces all three products from the same basic design, using design software to automatically adapt the design to specific market preferences.[9]

USER INTERFACES

Another key component of superior product design is the integration of the user interface into the core of the product design activities. Standardized electronics and components mean that it is product design that makes the function clear. Is it a camera or a phone? Is it a video game console or a DVD player? Increasingly, it is the product design and user interface alone that reveals the primary function.

As LCD screens have become widespread in even the simplest consumer electronics, the quality of user interfaces has declined significantly. Menu-driven UI approaches brought from the PC business have resulted in products that are clumsy to use and rich in useless functionality. The result is MP3 players without "Play" and "Pause" buttons where users must drill through multiple layers of menus to play their songs.

"Our return rates in the US are always much higher than in Europe," says Tin Wu, the Chief Executive of Cyberhome Entertainment, a fast-growing maker of consumer electronics. "In the US, if you can't figure it out without reading the manual, it's

---

9. Jordan, Miriam, Karp, Jonathan, "Machines for the Masses." *The Wall Street Journal,* December 9, 2003

likely that it will be returned. In Europe, they read the manual carefully, often before buying the product, as retail returns are much more difficult."

The payoff from integrating the physical design and user interface tightly can be substantial. In the case of Linksys, design improvements in routers and voice-over IP products for home users resulted in "significant" reductions in return rates. Apple's iPod is an example of what is possible from superior design, where it takes just one button press to start playing music. The iPod also contains a context-sensitive scroll wheel that performs multiple functions; however, the most common functions that users demand instant access to each have their own buttons.

As demonstrated by these companies, superior design requires a fundamentally different approach to design than what most electronics companies currently practice.

Design is no longer an afterthought but a key element driving the product design. Design has been given equal footing with software and electronics, resulting in a strong design influence in the final product. Processes are revamped to be highly integrated and collaborative. Stylists take the lead in capturing customer requirements and serve as the final arbiters of what is acceptable. Market intelligence and manufacturing expertise shape the look and feel of the final product as much as technological capabilities.

EXECUTING SUPERIOR DESIGN AND USER INTERFACES

In the electronics industry, however, design is more than a pretty package. A product must be functional as well as aesthetic. The color, shine, or shape of a mobile phone body may catch the consumer's eye, but this phone also must protect the internal components from wear and tear to earn the manufacturer repeat business. To design packaging that also meets rigid functional specifications, design tools must be tightly linked to analytical tools. But rapid changes in consumer tastes and demands are forcing companies to work at an extremely rapid pace. Global distribution complicates the equation, introducing enormous product variations and the need to manage them.

A key challenge in building a better design business process and infrastructure is achieving rapid customization without compromising time-to-market or quality. The only practical solution is to build multiple products on a common platform, enabling design reuse and morphing.

RAPID ITERATION

To achieve seamless blending of mechanical design with software and hardware engineering requires the ability to iterate rapidly, continually moving toward optimum design without sacrificing performance metrics (for example, rigidity, heat dissipation, and water resistance). Analysis and testing of designs against real-life requirements must be performed quickly and accurately, with the results fed back into the design and engineering chain. Increasingly, complex mathematical analysis must be performed at the earliest stages of design to meet critical—and increasingly narrow—market windows without sacrificing quality. Only the most sophisticated mechanical design systems support such cutting-edge requirements. Engineering data must be seamlessly linked to mould development to achieve the speed and accuracy required to enable the supply chain to deliver parts that are right the first time.

ORGANIZATIONAL INTEGRATION

In the case of user interface development, the key component is organizational integration of the user interface team with the mechanical, electronics, and software development functions. Product localization and customization are also integrated with user interface and mechanical design. In the mobile telephone market, for example, operators increasingly want to impose common physical packaging and software standards. A mobile phone network might want a special button, for example, that takes users to branded content online.

Unlike the electronics industry, automotive and aerospace manufacturers traditionally have focused heavily on mechanical design, including product styling. As a result, these industries have already developed sophisticated processes, process automation, and Product Lifecycle Management (PLM) tools that dramatically reduce the time required to develop products. These tools, which include solutions not only for exterior design but also for testing and manufacturing analysis for a large number of product variations using digital mock-ups, can be applied to the electronics industry as well.

Style-conscious companies don't have to build physical prototypes but instead can use digital mock-ups to engineer and test models and evaluate manufacturability. Strong mechanical design solutions allow companies to significantly reduce design cycle times while eliminating design errors that previously remained undetected until manufacturing began. These same solutions allow reuse of standard items and parts catalogs. Inventories of existing designs can be re-used as the starting point for new styles, enabling rapid morphing from the old product to the new. The system automatically adjusts all related parts and systems each time a change is made, facilitating customization of a single style for multiple markets. Analysis is performed early in the design cycle, speeding the team's arrival at an optimum combination of performance and look and feel. Some tools even allow designers themselves to perform basic analysis, facilitating early identification of the most promising design approaches.

MORE BEST PRACTICES

A few electronics companies have begun to apply these tools to their own competitive challenges. Audio powerhouse Clarion, for example, is focusing on continuing innovation and improvement of its product lines using PLM solutions. According to Toshiyuki Nakazaki, Clarion Malaysia's Director of Research and Development, establishing new market categories requires insight in recognizing consumer trends, a shorter product development turnaround time, and producing high-quality products. He adds,

"The adoption of PLM solutions has been instrumental in capturing, managing, and sharing corporate know-how."[10]

Similarly, Taiwan-based Acer Inc., a personal computer manufacturer, is using PLM tools to promote collaboration among its internal teams and suppliers. The solution automates all project, document, and product structure management as well as Bill of Materials (BOM) and workflow processes administration. Acer's IT Business Group follows a strategy it describes as "empowerment through innovation." This strategy is intended to keep Acer in a top position within the highly competitive worldwide IT industry by employing advanced collaboration systems to continually enhance the company's innovation competitiveness.[11]

RECOMMENDATIONS

Electronics companies that want to increase their competitive edge should consider upgrading their design capabilities and user interface development. As a first step, management should perform an analysis looking at the required key capabilities:

- Assess the skills required for implementing industry-leading design capability. Organizations that have made the transformation, including Apple and Samsung, typically have needed to increase staffing levels and upgrade staff skills.

- Assess the organizational alignment to position design on a par with other development teams. Realignment will take reorganization and process changes.

- Review business processes so that when integrated, mechanical, electrical, and software and user interface design activities come together in a competitive cycle timing. An integrated framework will ease the transition.

10. "Clarion Accelerates Product Development with PLM Technologies." IBM case history, 2003.
11. "Acer Inc. Seeks Shortest Time-to-Market in Industry with Product Lifecycle Management Solutions from IBM and Dassault Systems." IBM press release, January 2004.

■   Identify the number of derivative products that can be successfully launched from a single platform. Help ensure that design analysis tools can keep pace with variations, each of which must be individually tested.

■   Assess infrastructures for mechanical design. The newest tools have significant productivity advantages over older systems and leverage best-in-class capabilities developed originally for the automotive and aerospace industries.

■   Assess infrastructure for user interface development globally. Usability is often regional and cultural. Best-in-class looks at usability both globally and locally in developing product.

These actions will help position companies to make the transformation into companies that are driven by product design and responsive to market demands.

CONCLUSION

Electronics companies' use of product and user interface design to gain competitive advantage requires an iterative process that adds steps to the typical product development process. The give-and-take between design and mechanical design and electronics engineering must be ongoing, without lengthening design cycles. In fact, modern tools and processes that accommodate a highly iterative process serve to reduce design cycles while increasing innovation. Electronics manufacturers now have a chance to apply these proven processes to their competitive challenges. By doing so, electronics companies can be more

■   Focused on consumer preferences.

■   Responsive to market dynamics.

■   Variable in product options offered.

■   Resilient in the face of rapidly shifting consumer preferences.

Product design, of course, is not a substitute for other measures of quality, such as features, functions, durability, and reliability. But design does provide another choice for consumers, and it's one the marketplace has embraced. It's proven that consumers today pass over less stylish offerings and willingly pay a substantial premium for stylish products.[12] Therefore, electronics companies that want to gain a competitive edge today should shift their focus to product design choices for consumers.

Few markets are more competitive than the electronics industry. The differentiation that can be achieved through superior product design can result in dramatic payoffs: more reliable demand, pricing premiums, lower return rates, and soaring brand value. Given the average margins in consumer electronics and the huge volumes, even modest improvements in price premiums or lower return rates are the difference between losing money and making money.

12. IBM Business Consulting Services analysis, 2004.

12

Consumer Relationships: A Tale of Channels and Brands

Sean Lafferty, Brigitte Majewski

In this new millennium, demand for consumer electronics is hot—plasma TVs, camera phones, and MP3 players are the "I can't live without it" status symbols of our age. Who would benefit most from this trend than the global consumer electronics player? Indeed, after a rough start to the decade, CE manufacturers are seeing a revenue rebound. What they are not seeing is improved profits. A strategic analysis shows CE players in an uncomfortable position, sandwiched between hyper-competitive retailers serving savvy consumer, and low-cost new entrants leveraging cheap labor and less overhead. Only CE manufacturers who re-evaluate their relationship with the end-user to bring solutions and not just boxes to market will secure profits. This is a dramatic change from today and represents the customer-centric era in CE manufacturing.

This chapter looks at the recent financial trends in the CE industry to highlight the increasing revenue/stifled profit paradox. We assess the convergence of marketplace developments, including the entrance of low-cost players, an increase in retailer and consumer power, and shortening product lifecycle. Finally, we recommend customer-centric strategies that CE manufacturers can consider to revitalize their operating margins.

THE SCENARIO

Where is the consumer electronics industry headed? What will the next five years look like? Before we get out our crystal ball to predict the future, let's look at the past five years and pick out some of the trends that are likely to continue into the near future. One way to look back at the CE industry would be from the perspective of an Economics professor who might say, "The last five years were an era of intense competition spurred by emerging technology and productivity improvements."

Industry insiders might say, "The last five years were a bloodbath."

DECLINING PROFIT MARGINS

The most telling statistic over the past five years is the industry-wide decline in profit margins for traditional consumer electronics manufacturers.

In fact, from 2000 to 2002, the average net profit margin for the top 10 CE players dropped from 6 percent down to 2 percent.[1]

The decline was probably brought on largely from many of the same macroeconomic factors that brought discretionary spending down for the average consumer.

To stop the bleeding, the CE industry went into cost-cutting mode. All of the major CE manufacturers underwent massive workforce reductions and leveraged technology to drive efficiencies in the supply chain and manufacturing.

As a result of that cost-cutting splurge, the industry's average margins recovered to about 4 percent in 2003. However, this is still

---

1. IBM analysis of Factiva data.

down from the historical norms of 6 percent or better, and there is little room to slash more cost out of operations for most of the major players.

Not surprisingly, the stock markets were efficient and severely punished the CE players even more than most other sectors. From 2000 to 2003, the top five CE companies lost between 30 and 70 percent of their total market capitalization. In 2004, we saw a slowing of the market cap destruction as revenues began to show some signs of improvement.

THE ROAD TO RECOVERY?

The year 2004 was a landmark in which revenue growth in consumer electronics returned to its highest level in nearly five years. The CEA estimates that consumer electronics factory sales soared by 10.7 percent in 2004 to an all-time record $113.5 billion (Figure 12.1) and predicts an equally strong growth rate in store for 2005, with sales also climbing 10.7 percent to $125.7 billion.[2]

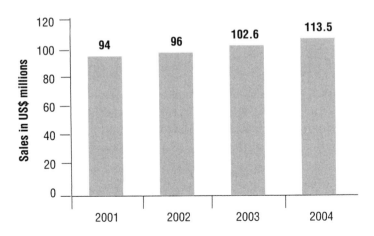

Figure 12.1 Revenue of consumer electronics companies in the US ($B 2001–2004).

---

2.   "CEA Says '05 Sales Will Grow 10.7 Percent'" *TWICE*, January 24, 2004.

But still, profit margins in 2004 only remained relatively low at about 4 percent on average across the major players.

It is quite the paradox—revenue growth got hot, hot, hot, and yet it was still incredibly difficult to make a profit. A look behind the revenue numbers showed that the gains came entirely from huge increases in unit volumes, and a continuing drop in average unit prices. NPD Consumer Electronics Price Watch reports that their standard basket of CE goods dropped in price by nearly 40 percent from $16,999 in January 2003 to $10,825 in January 2005[3] (Figure 12.2). Why is this happening?

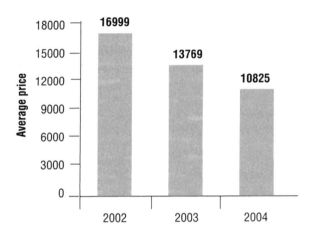

Figure 12.2   Average price of NPD's consumer electronics basket (US$) 2002–2004.

RETAILER POWER AND INCREASED CONSUMER BUYING POWER

The past five years have shown us a change in the relationship among manufacturers, retailers, and consumers. What seems to have happened is this: By scaling up, the successful retailers are aggregating more consumers into a single buying channel. This affords them immense bargaining power with the CE manufacturers, which in turn leads to the manufacturers slashing their prices

3.   NPD Consumer Electronics Price Watch, February 2005.

in an effort to maintain manufacturing volumes. If the manufacturers do not meet the price points that consumers want, and the retailers enforce, then the retailers turn to low-cost knockoffs.

There are several reasons for this to have happened.

Hyper-competition among retailers has created a tough set of buyers for CE manufacturers. Retailers with diluted value propositions rarely stay in business. We've seen Gateway fold up shop, Sears and Kmart merge to stay afloat, and Circuit City manage rumors of an acquisition. It's likely that geographic expansion will result in even further consolidation at the global level. Left standing were focused, powerful companies that own the customer relationship.

Before any kind of steady state could be achieved, however, high price points attracted large, powerful competitors such as Target, Wal-Mart, and price clubs who cater to the value priced shopper. This all acknowledges increase in consumer buying power. Wal-Mart became the second largest retailer of CE products in 2002, growing at more than 13 percent.[4] By 2003, the top three retailers in CE were Wal-Mart, Circuit City, and Best Buy, accounting for more than $48 billion in US sales in 2004.[5]

By contrast, the largest specialty retailers that command higher prices by offering the consumer detailed product knowledge, Electronics Boutique and Tweeter, accounted for less than $2 billion in combined sales.[6]

ATTACK OF THE UNBRANDED MANUFACTURERS

Low-cost technology copy-cats have always nipped at the heels of the truly innovative consumer electronics companies by making similar products much cheaper.

However, advances in digital technology have made it much easier to duplicate new technologies, and advances in productivity have

---

4. "Electronics Retailers Top $100B In Sales." *Forbes,* January 12, 2003.
5. "The TWICE Top 100 Retailers of Consumer Electronics & Major Appliances," *TWICE*, November 22, 2004.
6. Ibid.

increased the speed with which the low-cost players can duplicate innovative products. Furthermore, the retailers have excelled in diminishing the power of the brand at the time of purchase.

In the period from 2001 to 2004, China became the new source for many new low-cost brands that made inroads with major retailers. For example, the low-cost player Apex Digital Inc. was founded in 1999 with a focus on the DVD market. According to *The New York Times*, Apex led the charge to the $29 DVD player in the US, driving more than $1 billion in sales in 2003.[7] Apex was able to achieve such pricing because it could manufacture and distribute DVD players worldwide employing a mere 100 people and sourcing all labour to Jiangsu, China. By 2002, Apex reported its presence in over 20,000 retail outlets in the United States. With lower labor and overhead costs than European and Japanese counterparts, these Chinese and Korean players have a significant cost advantage.

Apex is not an isolated example. In fact, Circuit City, in 2005, carries 20 different brands of DVD players alone in their online store. In the newer Flat Panel TV segment, they already carry 19 different brands.

The retailers have supported the brand position of these low-cost products by making it harder for consumers to distinguish between the major players and the imitators. In many retail stores, products are displayed in a very uniform fashion with small black and white tags that tell the consumer little more than the name of the brand, the price and maybe a couple of cryptic feature descriptions. If that is not enough to persuade the consumer that the brand means very little, the salesman's pitch, "This one is made in the same factory as that name brand," will probably sway a customer to a lower priced/higher margin brand.

Plus, with prices dropping faster than ever, consumers do not care if something better will come out next year. They'll just buy another one later. Consider digital cameras, which are on their second adoption phase, where early adopters are buying higher

---

7.   "The Way We Live Now," *The New York Times*, July 3, 2004.

megapixel models for less than $100 per megapixel. Consumers want it now, and they want it cheap.

THE TRENDS GOING FORWARD

With that glance backward out of the way, let's now look at the trends that are likely to continue for the *next* five years and that will put the CE industry out of the profit slump and onto a growth path.

SHORTENING PRODUCT LIFECYCLE OR INCREASED ADOPTION?

The traditional model for CE manufacturers says that they would command a price premium on new products while their competition scrambled to create new and better products. CE was once much like the pharmaceutical industry still is today. Once an original equipment manufacturer (OEM) got ahead on a particular technology, it would enjoy years of dominance and high margins to recover its investment in the technology and also pay for research into new areas.

But today, the fast followers have gotten so fast at duplicating new technologies that the premium price period has dropped from years to months.

Is the glass half empty or half full? If the glass is half full, one might say that consumers are savvier than ever and are willing to adopt new technologies more rapidly than ever. Therefore, rapid revenue growth during the high-margin introduction period for new products is achievable. If the glass is half empty, one might say that profits are harder to capture in consumer electronics because the lifecycle of new products has shortened, and therefore products commoditize and prices drop too quickly to overcome the development cost of new products.

Either way, the fact remains that consumers are adopting technology more rapidly, product lifecycles are shortening, and therefore the high-profit portion of the lifecycle represents a larger and shorter opportunity.

The shortened technology lifecycle in consumer electronics was first witnessed with the DVD player. DVD players first hit the shelves in 1995, and by 2001 the industry had already reached 10 million units sold, just six years later. The average unit selling price dropped an astounding 63 percent from $800 to $300 in that same time frame. The price dropped another 58 percent to $125 in the next three years and by 2004, the average unit selling price had reached $42. The DVD industry shook the foundation of the CE industry as it signalled a new business model where the highly profitable early stages of the product lifecycle were shortened. If digital optical technology could become commoditized so quickly, what technologies could possibly be safe? See Figure 12.3.

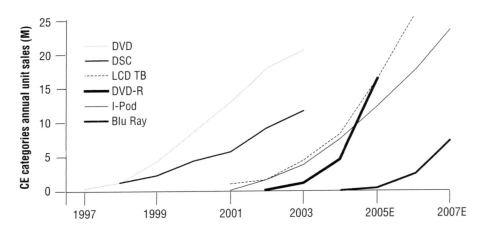

Figure 12.3 CE categories annual unit sales (millions).

Today, Apple is grappling with the same phenomenon. The iPod surprised the market and took it by storm in October 2002. By January of 2005, Apple had already sold 10 million units, achieving in less than three years what the entire DVD industry did in six years. However, despite having huge competitive advantages in design, software, technology, and integration with services, the iPod has already come under attack just two years later by Sony and others. In 2004, iPod was forced to drive its average prices down by from $367/unit to $296/unit, a nearly 25 percent drop. Apple further fended off the competition by slashing prices another 20 percent at the onset of 2005 as it introduced a variety of product features and hit nearly every price point in the music player market, further indicating the maturity of the product.

By 2011, this premium price period will shrink even further.

RETAILERS WIDEN THE GAP

CE players also can expect retailers to move closer to the end user through improved services in an effort to combat the price erosion they themselves created.

Retailers are gathering billions of terabytes of customer data to improve the overall customer experience—from localization of merchandise to letting shoppers return to the store products they bought online. Best Buy announced a formal Customer Centricity Plan (focus on best customers) and focus on services; Circuit City offers a cash back card; and RadioShack is revamping stores. These programs tap into earnings, and retailers will pass the cost of loyalty programs, cash back cards, multiple service offerings, and cool venues not onto the customer but to the CE manufacturer.

Retailers have begun counting the number of shoppers who enter the doors to compare to the number of transactions made in a day. Retailers are using cameras and "hot floors" to map customer shopping paths to identify roadblocks and high traffic areas. Retailers sponsor documentaries that follow potential shoppers around for months until they decide to buy—to capture the true buying process.

The net result is that CE manufacturers are in a position to sell to large, powerful retailers who can dictate how, when, and where the end user sees, feels, and buys the CE manufacturer's goods.

CE players can expect their retailers to continue to push for lower prices as retailer competition forces increasing costs to sell. CE players who don't comply will find an increasing portion of their shelf space handed over to cheaper OEMs.

In some ways, it does not seem intuitive that Sony, Panasonic, and Samsung—powerful brands built upon legacies of innovation and product breadth—may be forced to kowtow to merchants.

But the phenomena is a reflection of what is going on with the retailers who are in turn kowtowing to customers whose power has grown dramatically in the last decade with the Internet's information sharing and price transparency.

ONLINE CE SUPER SHOPPERS

The Internet is an increasingly important sales channel for the CE industry, and you might even say that it is the critical channel that is causing a lot of the changes you see happening.

Online sales continue to grow as Internet and broadband adoption increases. Consumers feel more comfortable with the security of online transactions, and consumers are getting accustomed to thinking first of shopping online instead of traveling to the nearest mall.

In 2003, 15 percent of CE shoppers reported that online stores were their preferred point of purchase,[8] and online sales of CE products is forecast to reach 30 percent of total industry sales by 2008.[9] This may seem like a high estimate, but by comparison, the PC industry is already at 50 percent.

Sales are one very important measure, but perhaps more important is that 50 percent of all purchases are already researched online, with manufacturers Web sites listed as one of the primary resources. Shoppers have instant access to tools such as product reviews and price comparisons to help them match their wants and needs to the right product and then also find the best deal for that product. By 2011, it is likely that as many as 90 percent of all purchases will be researched online prior to the purchase, with as much as 30 percent

---

8. Consumer Electronics Association, www.ce.org.
9. Omwando, Helen, "How To Sell Consumer Electronics Online," *Forrester,* June 4, 2004.

of the purchase volume online. For manufacturers, 75 percent of all CE purchases will be researched on their Web sites, and 10 percent of purchases will be online direct from the manufacturer.

As the consumer comfort level with the online shopping channel grows, shoppers begin to distinguish brands by electronics category. Gone are the days when consumers bought all their components from one manufacturer. Now more consumers are comfortable mixing and matching to meet their own needs. At the same time, CE manufacturers continue to maintain wide, expensive product lines composed of several underperforming categories to cater to ever dwindling loyalists. Consider that consumers tend to recognize most CE brands, but very few brand names recur in unsolicited name recollection. The retailer's value proposition, to carry a broad line of brands, doesn't help.

WHAT TO DO ABOUT IT?

How should a player in the CE industry prepare for swimming in the increasingly turbulent waters that the next five years will bring?

THE IMPORTANCE OF "HIT PRODUCTS"

The shortening lifecycle phenomenon intensifies the importance of "hit products" in today's market.

In the old model, the manufacturer could count on years of high margins to recover the cost of research and development. Today, that is no longer the case.

By 2011, CE manufacturers will have to launch innovative new hit product categories every 18 months to be profitable.

This means that development lead times have to be cut drastically.

And while the processes to create new, innovative products have already been improved, those processes to create innovative products still need to get better in order to meet the challenge of the future.

Not only do the hits have to come more frequently, but manufacturers can't afford major missteps with unsuccessful product lines. Every innovative new product category developed by the CE manufacturers has to be a hit. Whether it is the next generation of the connected home or the ultimate converged portable device, manufacturers need the product to boom like the iPod.

But how can manufacturers know what the next iPod is going to be? To get a higher rate of hit products, the OEMs will have to get better at predicting their customer's wants and needs.

This type of thinking has to be present throughout the entire organization. Take Samsung, for example. Samsung has developed a reputation for leading the CE industry in understanding the customer and designing and marketing effectively to that customer. In fact, Samsung has embedded the customer-driven focus far deeper into its organization.

GETTING CLOSER TO THE CUSTOMER

CE players have already been battling back against the retailers to get to know the customer better and own a big part of the customer relationship. If the manufacturer has a deep enough relationship with the customer, the manufacturer will be able to predict the customer's wants and needs and can take back control of the CE value chain.

But before building the relationship with the customer, it is critical that the manufacturers know who their target customers are. Step one in getting to know the customer is to identify your best customer. What are their basic demographics? How do they prefer to shop? What CE do they already own? What CE do they plan to buy next? Where do they do their research? Where do they shop? What else do they buy? What are their pet peeves when shopping for CE? What triggers them to buy? Why do they buy your product over other products?

These are hard questions to answer. You may not even be able to easily answer these questions about your own shopping habits—or worse, your answers differ from your actual behaviour.

Getting these insights requires a dedication and investment in customer research. We are not talking about just surveys and focus groups but gathering real data at the point of execution.

Sure, retailers may own the customer experience today, but CE players have plenty of opportunities to gather their own unique insights. Most shoppers spend a good deal of time researching expensive products before purchase. The more useful information CE players provide about their products, the more likely the shopper is to use them as a resource. And if the consumer comes to your site, you have the chance to build a relationship with them.

The key is to know what the consumer thinks is useful. Most CE manufacturer Web sites to this day do a poor job on even basic tasks like explaining what's included, what accessories are needed, and compatibility. Consumers are looking for the manufacturer to be the expert on its own products. With the right Web monitoring in place, manufacturers can see what products are hot (high hit rates) and what products tend to underwhelm (high drop-off rates).

But there is another channel the manufacturer can use, one that could be a better predictor of their customers' wants and needs than even the data from their customer's online Web activity. The manufacturer has a wealth of customer data residing in its service centres.

CE companies would get a long way by addressing problem calls with more of a customer service approach and gathering data in the process. Every service call could require the service provided to gather basic information about the customer and how they were using the product—where did they buy it, what room was it in, who used it, for what main purpose? This data set could be shared with product design and marketing.

And taking the opportunity to apologize for any product issues goes a long way to building customer trust and loyalty. A short apology and thank you e-mail after every service call, along with a small gift card to the direct store or preferred partner retailer, would be a lot cheaper than trying to regain that customer once they've sworn off your products for life.

BUYING CUSTOMER BASES

In addition to bringing together internal data sources, CE manu-facturers are also buying customers. An example of this is HP's photo imaging group's 2005 purchase of Snapfish, an online photo-finishing service. While the photo-finishing business is growing at more than 50 percent per year, its revenues will account for less than 1 percent of HP's total topline number. However, the real asset that HP acquired is the relationship with more than 13 mil-lion digital camera users. These are consumers who choose to come and visit the Web site, freely give personal information to the service provider, and are savvy online users. By having access to this valuable customer base, HP can test product ideas and also market new photo-related products directly to the customer.

PARTNERING FOR CUSTOMER BASES

Yet another way to get closer to the customer is to find alternate value chains that cater to your same customer base. Panasonic is a great example of this (see Partnering Case Study: Panasonic, below). Rather than trying to build a new base or invest huge sums of money to acquire businesses with big customer bases, Panasonic has gone into partnerships with a variety of companies that have large customer bases to access.

PARTNERING CASE STUDY: PANASONIC

Consumer electronics leader Panasonic has addressed customer centricity by enhancing the services available for its products. This includes creating an option to serve the four percent of consumers who choose to buy direct from the manufacturer. To do more than just setting up a Web site or providing a phone number, they have been taking a fresh approach to dealing with end users. Panasonic did this by reconsidering how consumers really realize the benefit of Panasonic products. A small, effective team in the US then developed value networks around that total experience.

Panasonic is reaching out to meet its consumers where they want to purchase, even in the direct channel. By deconstructing who the consumer turns to at various points in the shopping and ownership cycle, Panasonic identified partners who best complement Panasonic's overall value proposition.

Consider the purchase process: Panasonic is the market leader for the plasma TV, consistently holding the number-one position in US retail plasma TV sales for most of 2005 to date. Even with falling prices, a plasma purchase represents a serious financial commitment for the average consumer—one would be hard pressed to find a quality unit under $5,000 at the time of print. For consumers who want to participate in customer loyalty programs, Panasonic partnered with American Express to offer double points for any online purchase made using an eligible, enrolled American Express Card. To meet its consumers need for financing, the company developed its own payment alternative, the Panasonic Direct Credit Card, powered by GE with promotional financing such as no interest, no payment for 12 months. Eventually this card could also be used at participating retailers. These options complete the direct purchasing solution for the consumer by connecting with American Express' loyalty program or freeing up the buyer's cash for a whole year.

Another critical component to enjoying one's plasma TV is convenient access to content—and it works the other way around: The best way to enjoy on-demand action adventure and comedies is on a colour-perfect plasma TV. That synergy brought about a successful partnership between Panasonic and local cable companies. Select cable company subscribers now enjoy rebates on Panasonic purchases made through the cable companies' online stores. Cable companies obtain a new mechanism in their battle for share against satellite-based TV reception, and Panasonic enables its consumers who want to buy direct to do so.

continues

In addition to providing the consumer with a direct-from-the-manufacturer purchasing solution, these partnerships also provide the opportunity to reach out to other customers who fit Panasonic's target market. Credit card companies have extensive databases on customers whose profiles can be sliced and diced any number of ways to procure the ideal mailing list. Cable companies have millions of subscribers who receive monthly statements or log on to cable broadband Web sites, both vehicles ripe for cross-marketing. Future opportunities could include product placement in cable programming and discounts on Panasonic products with every new cable subscription. Imagine a partnership where new home construction comes with the option for a wall-mounted, cable-ready plasma TV already financed into a GE home mortgage. With new avenues available for consumers to learn about and enjoy Panasonic products, the manufacturer becomes closer to the end user.

Strategically, Panasonic has developed a core competency in partnership development. From identifying the best partners, to contract negotiation, to program design and implementation, to post-execution communication strategy, Panasonic is shifting from linear value chains to more flexible value webs. Even on the back-end, Panasonic has partnered with Digital Alliance Corporation for customer service, Shutterfly for online photo processing, IBM for IT work, and Installs Inc. for professional installation of key products. Net result: Panasonic becomes the hub through which the end customer redeems the full electronics entertainment experience—product, financing, installation, content, and more—without having to make the costly buy or build investment. The consumer values the Panasonic product more because of the completeness of the solution provided by Panasonic and the flexibility to make the purchase in the consumers preferred channel.

But are these partnerships working? Annual sales through Panasonic Direct, Panasonic's key eCommerce channel, say yes. Weekly sales for 2005 have been two to three times that of the same week in 2004. May 2005 sales, typically reflective of a seasonal drop, beat last year's traditional seasonal peak of November 2004. Phoned-in inquiries on Panasonic product are up dramatically, and Web site hits grow weekly. For the US consumer who is looking for a customer–centric sales and ownership experience, Panasonic has successfully partnered to bring more value.

SOLUTIONS FOCUS

When the manufacturers gain access to the consumer, they need to capitalize on that access by understanding their wants and needs. The hit product of the future is not only about emerging technology innovations. Innovation that matters solves a consumer want or need—it is a complete solution.

The complete solution includes everything to make the device or devices come to life, including the content services, product support services, purchase transaction support, alternative channels, and the right accessories to help the consumer get the most out of the product.

For example, what good is a portable music player without legal, easy, and cost-effective access to songs? What good is a game device without the games? What good is a digital camera without being able to print and distribute the photos? Manufacturers will increasingly need to ensure that these services are available and easy for the consumer to use, particularly with the manufacturer's devices.

Additionally, consumers expect the manufacturer to make the purchase transaction easy to complete. This is coming in the form of financing options available either at the retail outlet or direct from the manufacturer. The shopper is demanding more and better information about the product online. Online chats with informed sales representatives and access to well-informed call centers will only become more critical to equipping the consumer with the knowledge they need to make the CE purchase.

This expected level of support extends beyond the sale into after sales. Consumers expect products to work easily and also expect to have issues resolved quickly and without hassle. Online self-service, call centres, and in-the-box documentation become increasingly important as the technology in the hands of consumers becomes increasingly complex.

Consumers will shop where they want to shop, when they want to shop. The traditional retail channel will continue to be the dominant channel, but the trend toward online shopping for CE is undeniable. Additionally, the number of consumers who want to deal directly with the manufacturer will continue to rise. It is imperative for the CE manufacturers to meet the consumer wherever they may shop. Trying to sell direct while maintaining strong relationships with retailers will remain a delicate balancing act for the manufacturers, but one that they have no choice but to embrace. Otherwise, the industry remains susceptible to direct-selling infiltrators like Gateway who rocketed past Sony, Panasonic, and Samsung to grab the #1 share in the Plasma market in 2003.[10]

CONCLUSION

Just as JuBock Ryu, Engagement Partner for Samsung at IBM BCS, summarizes, "It is the Market Driven Company that shows superior ability to understand, attract, and keep valuable customers."

Over the next five years then, you will most likely see these things happening in the CE industry:

---

10. "Gateway Becomes Top US Seller of Plasma TVs," *Digital-Lifestyles,* Sept. 25, 2003.

- Manufacturers will increase the number of new products launched, and a "hit product" will emerge every 18 months through 2011.

- Traditional manufacturers will focus more than ever on the end consumer by aggregating their knowledge from internal sources as well as acquiring and partnering to reach new consumers externally.

- Manufacturers will develop complete solutions for the consumer, rather than just new products. Solutions will include financing, purchase support, product support, and content services as well as accessories.

- Manufacturers will continue to increase their presence in the direct sales channel to meet the consumers who shop there, lowering the risk of an industry outsider coming in.

Consumer electronics manufacturers are shifting their focus from electronics to the consumer. In 2011, the players that do that successfully will thrive. The players that don't will be gone.

CHAPTER

13

Consumer Electronics in China in Year 2011

Albert Li

Things have changed dramatically in China in the last 25 years, and the story of the piano-playing Kong shows you just how much.

As early as the 1970s during China's Cultural Revolution, a little boy named Kong was coached by his mother to learn to play the piano. Twenty-five years later, Kong has turned out to be a world-class performing artist playing classical music all over the world, which is a success against the odds for any piano player. However, as a boy in Shanghai, Kong learned to play the piano without ever using a piano. His family could not afford one.

During that turbulent time in China's history, Kong's family was deprived of materialistic leisure products, even though music probably should have been classified as spiritual. The family could not own any musical instrument. However, Kong's mother would not sacrifice her son's artistic talent, and she drew a piano keyboard on cardboard paper to teach him to touch the white and black keys while she hummed the corresponding notes to him.

Kong has not forgotten his childhood hardships and recently returned to Shanghai to start the Kong Musical Education Foundation, whose vision is "to increase the musical population in China." An obstacle Kong needed to overcome was the high cost of a musical instrument in China.

The solution was a US $50 electronic full-size piano keyboard with earphone output. To fit this instrument onto small desks in small homes, it is also designed to be rolled up like a scroll for easy mobility and storage. And to show how much the world had changed in 25 years, Kong was able to get these scrollable pianos from a manufacturer just outside of Shanghai.

There are two points to Kong's story. China is now a major manufacturer of electronics goods—but China is a major consumer as well.

Since the mid-1990s, China has been the production hotbed of consumer electronics gears of DVDs, hi-fi, mobile phones, printers, accessories, desktops, and notebook computers. In fact, some 60 percent of China's annual electronic gears output of US $250 billion in 2004 were exported, and it is growing at 35 percent rate (Figures 13.1 and 13.2).[1]

This phenomenal growth was first ignited by Hong Kong's manufacturers in the 1980s who moved their factories into South China to make room for Hong Kong's booming real estate market and also to take advantage of low labor rates in China—at just about the time that China was coming out of the turbulent Cultural Revolution. By the 1990s, Taiwan manufacturers also started the mass exodus of production capacity from Taiwan into China to lower costs to compete in the global contract manufacturing business.

---

1. China Economic Statistics Monthly Express 2000-2004; *China Electronics Journal,* March 4, 2005, and Xie Ken, "China IT Market Forecast, 2002-2007," IDC, February 4, 2004.

The upstream suppliers of Printed Circuit Boards, IC packaging, enclosures, and mechanical assemblies followed suit to build factories in China so they could stay close to these contract manufacturers for just-in-time delivery and savings in transportation costs, as well as being attracted by the lower cost of the Chinese workers!

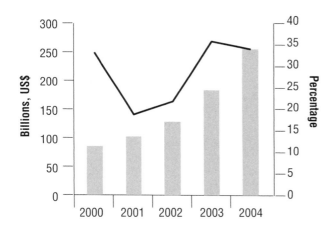

Figure 13.1 China electronics industry, 2000-2004, revenue and growth.

BKey Points

Key Industry Segments	• PC • Electronics component • Telecom equipment	75% of total sales revenue
Foreign Investment	• FIEs, TW, and HK companies entered China market for domestic market and lower manufacturing cost	77% of total sales revenue
Export Driven	• China as the manufacturing base in the global electronics value chain	60% of total sales revenue
Domestic Market	• IT investment is one of the key drivers of domestic demand	15.3% growth for the next 5 years

Figure 13.2 Key points impacting China's market.

Consequently, an ecosystem of component makers, contract manufacturers, and recently design houses and Chinese brand OEMs has emerged.

CHINA AS A MARKET

The selection on July 13, 2001, of Beijing as the host of the 2008 Olympic Games may have been the turning point for the world in realizing that China is not just a factory for assembling electronics goods for the affluent consumers in the West, but a huge market by itself.

With China's Gross Domestic Product growing at an average annual rate of 9.3 percent from 1900 to 2004,[2] it is not difficult to imagine the expanding middle class population of growing affluence and sophistication, by 2008, to be sipping coolers in their climate-controlled suburban homes watching Plasma or LED giant-screen television programs beamed through WiFi transmitters, while their newly born *second* child (yes, China may just have to change its single-child policy in view of a rapidly aging population) is being monitored by a sensor to alert the parents via the home's integrated network, just in case.

Increased income, the possibility of two-children families, and the quest for new knowledge to learn more about China itself and the world adds up to demand for many desktops, mobile phones, content downloads, and personal health, safety, and communication gear.

And the driver of the new consumer electronics market in China is no longer just affordability and low cost. It is also motivated by social and other needs. Case in point is the scrollable piano Kong needed: It had to be a musical instrument at relatively low cost such that sponsors could afford to give to the children of migrant workers from rural counties working in the affluent cities of Shanghai, Beijing, Guangzhou, and Hangzhou to "increase the musical population," and these instruments needed to be able to fit into the small homes and made-shift desks of their users.

---

2.   Chinese government statistics.

THE LOCAL CE PLAYERS

Japanese and Western companies, maybe with the exception of Philips, have until recently ignored the low-end consumer electronics market in China. The channel to the consumers and provision of after-sales-services are largely controlled by local companies such as Haier, Lenovo, SVA, TCL, Midea, and so on. Japanese brands such as Sony, Panasonic, and Hitachi have concentrated on the high end of the market.

The Chinese brand OEMs have developed a model of collaboration with Taiwan contract manufacturers to source their products (for example, mobile phones from Compal to be made under Lenovo's label) and with Japanese companies on technology cooperation (for example, SVA in joint venture with Matsushita to make plasma televisions for distribution under the Panasonic label in China). The products are usually sold by the Chinese brand makers irrespective of brand names. For example, Lenovo, a subsidiary of Digital China, is the largest distributor of IT products in China, selling anything from Apple iPod, Cisco hubs, Cannon printers, or DVD drives to thousands of dealers across China.

In other words, Chinese companies would get access to technologies and new products but rarely would give up the distribution and channel control.

THE CHINESE ENGINEERING ADVANTAGE

The critical factor that has made the "Scrollable Piano Player" feasible is not just the availability of standardized components and low factory worker wages, but the abundant and low-cost engineers available in China.

An independent survey sponsored by the US Department of Labor Statistics[3] in 2004 estimated the average Chinese factory workers rates to be US $0.64 per hour as compared to US $2.97 per hour in the United States. China's rates are then barely 3% of the US's!

---

3.   Coy, Peter, "Just how cheap is Chinese Labor?" *BusinessWeek*, December 2, 2004.

Engineers' wages are typically 15 to 20 percent of those in the United States. Combined with the fact that some 300,000 engineering graduates are coming out of Chinese universities every year versus only about 60,000 in the US, China would have distinct advantage in developing and producing CE products.

With the large domestic market and low product development cost, one would ask what killer products the Chinese have come out for its masses and the world. As a starter, Chinese low-cost products have successfully "killed" the markets for DVDs, televisions, and microwave ovens. Washing machines may be next.

Chinese factories, managed by Taiwan contract manufacturing and Japanese subsidiary companies, are also churning out personal computers, printers, and digital cameras at such speed and with such rapid waves of price cuts that there is almost no profit margin left to anybody, only mounds of obsolete inventories and huge amount of uncollectible trade receivables as many intermediates go bankrupt in the process.

On the home front, more and more unique Chinese consumer products are available. In fact, there are quite a few local hit products used that are not widely known outside of Asia:

- A prayer machine, which is a recorder spin-off that continuously hums with harmonized voices of prayer and thankfulness to release the owner of such chore in his/her morning and evening prayer sessions.

- A heavy duty electronic mosquito snapper armed with a search light to electrocute the annoying bug commonly found in China's damp cities.

- A punter's handheld terminal provided by the Hong Kong Jockey Club to place bets anytime and anywhere.

- A portable radio that tunes into local TV stations to allow homemakers and second-shift workforce to catch that can't-be-missed ending of their favorite programs away from their sitting room.

- And, of course, the scrollable piano.

CHINA'S AMBITIONS

China's ambition in consumer electronics is simply not just to stay as a niche player to assemble products for multinational companies or overseas channels, while developing products for its domestic market.

Both consumer and hi-tech electronics are global businesses where economy of scale matters. Chinese companies have a clear mandate to gain global dominance in brand, distribution, product development, and low cost.

After sales, services is not that critical for some of today's highly reliable consumer electronics such as PDAs, hand phones, and cameras that are usually "replaced" rather than "repaired" whenever they break down.

Chinese companies have made some bold moves to ascend to global leadership. Having gained a solid advantage in cost leadership and command of the rapidly expanding domestic market, they are working toward completing the global dominance equation of the following:

- Establishing or acquiring a global brand name.
- Gaining access to global distribution channels.
- Enhancing product innovation and R&D capability.

With the rapid erosion of profits in most consumer and IT product markets, many multinational companies have opted to exit (not unlike what Japanese companies did in exiting from the memory ICs and LCD panel segments in the 1990s). The following sections cover some of the Chinese companies that have grabbed on to these opportunities to expand globally.

TCL

TCL, a Shenzhen-based company with Chinese government background, took the lead in 2004 by merging its multi-media subsidiary with the TV division of Thomson, forming the world's largest television production joint venture. The TCL-Thomson company will produce 18 million television sets annually, replacing Sony as the leading global television maker. The two companies combined their TV and DVD businesses, with TCL International holding 67 percent and Thomson 33 percent of the shares. TCL-Thomson promotes products under the brand of TCL in Asia and other new markets while selling "Thomson" and "RCA" products in the European and North American markets.

TCL completed another merger of its mobile phone subsidiary with Alcatel's mobile phone division in 2004 to form TCL-Alcatel Mobile Phone Company, of which it owned 55 percent, but TCL closed down the joint venture nine months later because it could not stop losses in the market. Alcatel decided to sell its 45 percent share to TCL at reduced prices, which led to a huge capital loss for TCL and also foiled TCL's strategy of buying into global technologies and brands.

LENOVO

Lenovo, China's number-one personal computer maker bought IBM's PC division in 2004. Lenovo paid IBM US $1.25 billion in the form of $600 million cash and 18.9 percent of Lenovo shares. The deal allows Lenovo to use the IBM name, including the THINK® brand for notebooks, for five years. This merger made Lenovo the third largest personal computing company in the world behind Dell and HP, and it also put it at the top of the pile in its home territory. The two companies will form a partnership, with Lenovo pushing forward with the PC business while IBM backs it up with its well-established global distribution systems, sales, and quality notebook branding. Going forward, IBM will sell Lenovo's IBM-branded PCs through its own network.

BEIJING ORIENTAL ELECTRONICS

Beijing Oriental Electronics, another electronics manufacturer with strong government ties, purchased the bankrupt Hydis LCD manufacturer in Korea in 2003 as its technology source to get into LCD manufacturing. Since then, BOE has also acquired controlling interest of 25.4 percent in downstream leading LCD Monitor maker TPV Technology to assure outlet for its LCD panel production. In 2005, TPV announced the takeover of Philips' existing OEM Monitor business, amounting to approximately US $2 billion. Upon completion of the transaction, TPV will become the world's largest PC monitor manufacturer, with annual volume well exceeding 35 million units.

SVA

SVA, a Shanghai-based electronics group owned by the Shanghai government, also invested US $400 million of its own money in forming a joint-venture with NEC to build a fifth-generation LCD production facility that cost more than US $1 billion. The SVA Group has been making about US $20 million annually largely through their holding of equity interests in joint ventures run by foreign companies in the past. The SVA-NEC joint venture is the first time the group takes a majority 65 percent ownership and direct management and betting the group's 20 years of cumulated profit to acquire this new technology.

BENQ

BenQ, a Taiwan company spin-off from the Acer group, announced in 2005 the takeover of Siemens' unprofitable mobile business division to become the fifth largest mobile phone maker. Munich-based Siemens has to pay BenQ, Taiwan's biggest handset maker, 250 million euros to take control of its mobile business unit.

These Chinese companies considered these acquisitions hard to come by opportunities for them to establish their brands and global distribution networks—instead of remaining as contract manufacturers with evaporating bottom lines, whose fate has been at the mercy of brand OEMs.

Contract manufacturing has become an increasingly tough business in which to succeed, even for companies who invented the business in the 1990's. Figure 13.3 shows that the Consumer Brands (Sony, Matsushita, Samsung, and Philips) did better than (did not fall as much as) Electronics Contract Manufacturers (Flextronics, Solectron, and CLS) in the past four years.

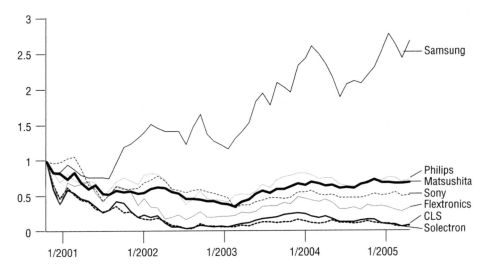

Figure 13.3 Relative share price performance of contract manufacturers versus brands.[4]

CAN CHINESE CE COMPANIES SUCCEED WITH GLOBALIZATION?

The Chinese consumer electronic companies are putting money where their mouths are in terms of acquisition and technology investment. With the likes of the IBM PC and the Thomson acquisition, they have certainly established the brand names and the

4. IBM analysis of Factiva data.

global distribution channel. The outstanding issues to international acclaim are the following:

- Can Chinese companies become innovative and come out with continuous new and exciting products?
- Can they manage a global enterprise of diverse culture and market dynamics far more complicated than a low-cost leader serving a monolithic Chinese market?

CHINESE R&D: THE INNOVATION QUESTION

With the Thomson TV and DVD mergers, TTE has acquired some impressive R&D facilities. But TTE Global Vice-President Mr Zhi Wen Ren admitted that "up to now, Chinese companies can only talk about our technology adaptation capability and not too much on technology culture. Our emphasis on technology and patents is not enough. Although we can use rapid technology adaptation to commercialize products, we are far behind in core technology and technology management."[5]

Nonetheless, TTE has made the ex-Thomson Indianapolis Lab its global research centre because it is relatively close to Silicon Valley and because it has developed strategic alliances and joint research programs with Intel, Texas Instruments, and Focus. TTE has also made its European research facilities a regional centre as it is an important contributing member on European digital TV standards. And TTE also kept the Industrial Design centre in Paris, as this centre has consistently won one to two "Top 100 Trendiest Consumer Products of the World" awards every year. Labs in Singapore and China are classified as Product Development Centers to commercialize products to markets in the most efficient, lowest cost, and quickest manner.

Speed and low cost seem to be the two dominant factors for Chinese companies with regard to product development, overriding technology, and functionality. Given this, technology leaders

---

5.   *CEO & CIO China*, June 5, 2005.

and patent holders would probably have no hesitation to come to companies such as TTE, SVA, and Lenovo for sharing and licensing of their crown jewels, as these Chinese companies provide a huge market, channel, and low cost to make their intellectual property valuable.

On speed to market, one anonymous Chinese executive has made the following observation: "Western companies usually take a deductive approach in product development in that they would define the most wanted product with all the possible bells and whistles designed in to sell to the early acquirers for good profit margins. Whereas Chinese companies typically launch very basic products at low cost, and then add more functionalities as the basic product got accepted by the market. It is an additive approach." The executive was describing the low-cost fast-adaptation approach once employed by Panasonic. But the issue in the case of TTE is now who to copy or adapt from!

THE FUTURE OF CHINA BRANDS

From a device standpoint, the consensus is that China is the dominant player in the 21st century, and branding is tilting to its side as well, aided by acquisition of global brands.

However, most of these devices are only re-branded or a customized version of OEM assemblies (LCD panels, PCB assemblies, disk drives, tape decks, and so on), which are made by even fewer component vendors such as Intel, Micron, and Corning on microprocessors, flash memories, and mother glass.

Is this the future of consumer electronics, or "electronic content and their hosting and provision?"

In retrospect, Thomson disposed of its money-losing consumer electronics TV and DVD devices division to focus on Media & Entertainment (M&E) services (such as publishing and distribution of DVD titles) and broadcasting and networking technologies. IBM's PC Division has been losing some 200 million a year for Big Blue. And Siemens even had to pay BenQ 250 million Euros to rid them of its money-losing Mobile Devices Unit. Not a pretty scene!

Winners of electronic content and network services hosting have not been declared yet, and the war has hardly begun.

ELECTRONIC CONTENT

China does not fall behind the competition in terms of the number of software engineers or Internet users in its population. In fact, China is the second largest Internet country in the world with 94 million users in 2005, after the US with 200 million users,[6] and is growing three times as fast. While this does not mean China produces electronic content at the same rate, the number will grow.

We do not anticipate that any dominant content creators are necessary in the media world, as this is work of individual authoring, where economy of scale should have no merit. With Chinese already the second most popular Internet language, Chinese electronic content will grow.

CONTENT HOSTING

There are many Chinese Internet directories and search engines in use, and the global players of Yahoo!, Google, eBay, and MSN are among them, but are not the most popular. Popular Web sites include the following:

- Baidu.com
- Chinasearch.com
- 3721.com
- Sina.com[7]
- Sohu.com
- Yeah.net[8]
- Yahoo China[9]

---

6. "Internet World Stats," *Miniwatts International,* www.internetworld-stats.com.
7. www.sina.com.cn.
8. www.163.com.
9. www.yahoo.com.cn.

Content hosting tends to be a regional or community play instead of a global play due to languages as well physical limitation to receive a shipment, visit a restaurant, or to meet a pal. Some of the sites listed here provide unique keyword service enabling Internet users to navigate the Web and search for relevant online information using real-world names and familiar identities in their native language, rather than having to remember cumbersome domain names. Some provide free premium email and even gateway for wireless short messaging.

CONCLUSION

For better or for worse, China has decided to take over the world's consumer electronics device manufacturing business because many others found it impossible to make that business profitable.

In fact, the Chinese may do the world the favor of standardizing the User Interface and Content Interface with continued research and development on mobility, usability, and 1:N connectivity to take a device that would connect seamlessly on the PC, in the car, on the stereo, to the PDA, mobile phone, and to the refrigerator LCD screens without the hassle of physically connecting the devices.

Electronic content and regional Internet services will continue to flourish from all over the world in a truly entrepreneurial fashion.

Yet innovation and global management skills are the two critical factors the Chinese need to overcome to be able to ascend to consumer electronics stardom in helping the world to enjoy life and to stay connected and healthy.

INDEX

Q–R